Dedication

We dedicate this book to our parents, Bud and Margaret Bousfield and Karl and Maxine Schultz, who masterfully nurtured seeds of faith in our lives.

And we also dedicate this to our son, Matt, who brings us down to earth every day and teaches us how to "receive the kingdom of God like a little child."

96904

Contents

Falling Along the Path

PAGE 18

Falling on Rocky Ground

PAGE 64

THE DIRT ON LEARNING

by Thom and Joani Schultz

Group
Loveland, Colorado

Credits
Editor: Paul Woods
Creative Development Editor: Dave Thornton
Copy Editor: Pamela Shoup
Art Director: Jean Bruns
Computer Graphic Artist: Joyce Douglas
Illustrator: Tom Clifton
Cover Art Director: Jeff A. Storm
Cover Illustrator: Gary Johnson
Production Manager: Peggy Naylor

Library of Congress Cataloging-in-Publication Data
Schultz, Thom.
    The dirt on learning / by Thom and Joani Schultz.
    p.   cm.
    Includes bibliographical references.
    ISBN 0-7644-2088-7 (alk. paper)
    1. Christian education--Teaching methods. 2. Sower (Parable)--Criticism, interpretation, etc. I. Schultz, Joani, 1953-   .
II. Title.
BV1534.S415   1999
268'.6--dc21   98-48888
                                                       CIP

10 9 8 7 6 5 4 3 2 1   08 07 06 05 04 03 02 01 00 99

Printed in the United States of America.

FALLING AMONG THORNS

PAGE 120

FALLING ON GOOD DIRT

PAGE 180

Introduction

You have discovered the most important treasure in the world. It will change your life dramatically. Indeed, it will save your life.

It is your faith in Jesus Christ.

What brought you to a knowledge, trust, and faith in Jesus was quite a miraculous process. The very hand of God reached out and touched you. And now, as a follower of Jesus Christ, you care deeply that those around you also experience this miraculous process.

Whether you're a teacher, pastor, youth worker, children's worker, parent, or friend, you've noticed that many can hear about the Prince of Peace, but relatively few trust him, follow him, and dedicate their lives to him. Most of those around you have heard the message, but they fail to understand. The message does not take root. Their lives do not change. They never experience the miraculous process that leads to life's most important relationship—the relationship with Jesus Christ.

How can some hear the message and believe, but others hear the same message and remain unaffected? While the process of faith may be miraculous, it is not entirely mysterious. Jesus himself explained the process. He revealed how some can hear the message but not understand, how some can receive the message with joy but later fall away, how some can hear the message but become distracted. And he explained how some hear the message, understand it, and transform into devoted followers.

What's the secret? In one of his stories Jesus divulged where we should look—in the dirt. A careful reading of the Parable of the Sower pulls our attention right down to earth, to ground level. The dirt is the main character in this intriguing story of faith. Getting to know this dirt can change everything you're doing to spread God's Word. So we invite you to put on a comfortable pair of old jeans and walk out into the field with us as we dig into *The Dirt on Learning*.

As you get your hands dirty in this process, we'd love to hear from you. Let us know your thoughts, discoveries, or questions. Contact us at:

Thom and Joani Schultz
Group Publishing
1515 Cascade Avenue
Loveland, CO 80538
E-mail: tschultz@grouppublishing.com
        jschultz@grouppublishing.com

Or visit this book's Internet Web site
(http://www.grouppublishing.com/dirt).

CHAPTER ONE

A Parable for Today

Daybreak creeps quietly across the South Dakota plains. The golden light reveals a green, yellow, and brown patchwork of family farms. Short, stocky Bud has already been awake and working for an hour—fueling the tractors, preparing the equipment, surveying the weather. This day begins quite like the last, and the one before that, and the one before that. For Bud, it's a routine he's practiced for fifty years.

He loves the routine and never tires of it. Every day he's a witness to countless miracles. The debut of the sun. The clouds' free delivery of life-giving raindrops. The birth of green sprouts from dormant seeds. The stalks' uncanny ability to manufacture perfect kernels of food.

As is his custom, Bud returns to the house for breakfast before heading out into the fields. Also quite customarily, a neighbor drops by to ask a favor and chat awhile.

The two compare overnight rainfall readings and sip a little coffee before the neighbor asks The Question. Bud's heard it a hundred times.

"How'd your corn do?"

This is the measuring stick for these farmers every harvest time. It's the score card, the numerical bushels-per-acre bottom line for a whole season of sweaty, dirty, before-dawn-to-after-dusk toil. This is the oh-so-simple number by which to measure the expertise, effectiveness, productivity, and wisdom of a South Dakota farmer.

"The year was pretty good to us," Bud says, searching for words to add his characteristic humility to his crop-yield score. Then he reveals The Answer.

The neighbor's eyes pinch to tight little slivers. He puts down his coffee cup and asks The Next Question. Bud's heard this one a hundred times too.

"Bud, how do you do it every year?"

Bud's "aw-shucks" reply chalks up his successful year to the weather and other elements beyond his control. But the neighbor knows that Bud's fields consistently outperform almost everyone else's because Bud knows the secrets. The secrets of successful farming.

What Bud knows about growing corn is what Jesus taught about growing disciples. It's an old, old process that still works today.

THE PARABLE OF THE FARMER

Bud's a real guy. He's Bud Bousfield, the real father of Joani, this book's co-author.

Like his South Dakota neighbors, we admire Bud's success in the world's oldest profession. (No, not *that* profession. See Genesis 2:15. The world's first job description has God commanding Adam to work the garden.)

The garden, the field, the farm have long been ideal metaphors for growing a living faith in God. Jesus preferred stories of seeds, fields, and harvests of grain and fruit, not only because they connected with his agrarian society, but because they illustrated so concisely a profound process. A process where listeners become hearers, where hearers become followers, where followers become disciples, where disciples make other disciples.

It seems no accident that the first parable in the book of Matthew is the Parable of the Sower (Matthew 13:1-23). The same parable also appears in Mark and Luke. The Gospels are filled with Jesus' intriguing stories that deliver spiritual truths through metaphors. Jesus used vivid comparisons to lead people from what they already knew to a new realm of understanding.

Some struggled with Jesus' stories. In fact, after this story of the sower, Jesus' own disciples came to him and asked, "Why do you speak to the people in parables?" This was a new approach for them—a new way of teaching. After explaining his intent, Jesus offered a clear explanation of the Parable of the Sower. Take note that Jesus only rarely explained the meaning of his parables. This parable was different. The Master did not want this one's meaning to blur. This one he sent to us with unmistakable clarity. This one was too crucial to leave to ambiguity.

His Story, Your Story

Jesus' tale begins with the sower scattering seeds about his field. Some seed falls along the path where it is quickly snatched by birds. Some seed falls on rocky ground where it withers and dies. Some seed falls among thorns where it eventually chokes. But other seed falls on good soil where it produces a plentiful crop.

What does this mean? Jesus explains:

● **The seed that falls along the path:** Some people will hear

God's message but not understand it. The evil one will snatch away what was sown in their hearts.

- **The seed that falls on rocky ground:** Some will receive the message with joy, but when trouble or persecution comes, they will fall away.

- **The seed that falls among thorns:** Some will hear the message, but will be choked by worries and the deceitfulness of wealth—desires for other things.

- **The seed that falls on good soil:** Some will hear the message, understand it, and produce abundant fruit.

This is a story for all who wish to spread the Word of God. In this one graphic story, we see a crisp picture of faith development—painted by the Son of God himself. It's an ageless story. Its searing examination of cause-and-effect is as profound today as it was when Jesus uttered it beside the lake. Make no mistake. This is God's story for us today.

If you wish to teach God's Word, this Parable of the Sower is your story. If you wish to preach God's Word, this is your story. If you wish to share God's Word with your own children and grandchildren, this is your story. If you wish to share God's Word with your neighbors, this is your story. If you wish to learn about God's Word yourself, grow in your faith, and bear much fruit, this is your story. Contained in this simple story are the stunning truths of the Master Teacher.

Spewing Seeds or Bearing Fruit?

Jesus crafts this story with deliberate overtones. Notice how Jesus emphasizes the *results* of the sowing. The focus is not on the sower, but on the ground and the results—the growth and fruit—of planting the seeds. The sower is not described. He is not critiqued for his seed-scattering style. He is not reviewed for his agricultural eloquence. The sower merely sows. But the solo sower produces four different results—three that lead to death and one that leads to life and abundance. Jesus makes very clear that the results are the crucial issue here. Only when seeds grow and bear fruit can the sower accomplish his purpose.

Don't miss this profound meaning for us today. Much like people in Jesus' day two thousand years ago, today's church needs to understand the emphasis of this story of the sower. Teachers, preachers, youth workers, children's ministers, and parents often miss the point. We tend to evaluate ourselves and others based solely on the quality, accuracy, passion, and learnedness of our message, what we consider the teaching. We're considered great sowers of the Word if we speak with authority. But Jesus' story illustrates that our success depends entirely on our seeds producing fruit. We can teach with great conviction, but unless our students learn and bear fruit, we really don't matter much.

Farmer Bud will tell you that the mere quality of a seed is no guarantee it will sprout. It can be an absolutely perfect seed in every respect. But more is required. He knows that other influences will affect the outcome of his crop. He knows that buying the best seed is only the beginning. He knows that how and where that seed is planted and how it's cared for are crucial to its eventual bearing of fruit. Simply spewing seeds will not make Bud a great farmer.

Unfortunately, today's church is built mostly upon the notion of seed-spewing. So long as seed is spewing, we feel good. We rarely analyze if people are learning, if any seeds are taking root. We practically never assess the effectiveness of different approaches, of different soils. And it rarely occurs to us to judge our effectiveness by the amount of fruit our people bear. But Jesus is calling us to look for more. He's asking, "How are you sowing? Upon what kind of ground are you attempting to farm? How must that ground be prepared in order to produce fruit? What's the magnitude of your harvest?" In the chapters ahead, we'll explore how to turn your emphasis from spewing to fruit-bearing, from mere teaching to genuine learning.

SAME SEEDS, DIFFERENT SOILS

Look how Jesus fixes our attention to the variety of soils. Here's another deliberate lesson for us. Identical seeds will not be received the same by all.

This is the salient factor that causes so much curiosity with Bud's neighbors. They know the exact type of seed he uses. They've tried using the same. But still their crops often don't produce the same bountiful yield as Bud's. How can that be? Many of Bud's secrets are found right in the Parable of the Sower.

Bud will tell you no two fields are alike. Their slopes and exposure to sun and prevailing weather patterns vary. The quality and consistency of their soils vary. Some fields are more "tired" than others; their nutrients have been drained. Some require more fertilizer. Others require more water than the average. Some are more prone to rocks and weeds.

The parable delivers the message that not all hearers of the Word will respond the same. They have different characteristics, different backgrounds, different makeup, different personalities, different ways in which they learn. If we wish to be successful with them, we must understand these differences. Like a good farmer, we can use the same good seeds. But we may need to customize, individualize how we sow, how we alter the growing environment,

THE DIRT ON LEARNING

how we nurture the seeds.

Many Christian folk today seem to believe one approach to learning and faith development will work for everybody. "God and his Word are the same yesterday, today, and tomorrow," they say. Yes, God is the same. But his people are as different as the South Dakota fields. That's the way God created them. Jesus' parable calls us to understand the variety in human makeup and response. The more we understand and tailor our approaches to this variety, the more effective we'll be.

The chapters ahead will supply lots of strategies for understanding and customizing your approaches with different kinds of students. And we'll give you an intriguing peek inside the human brain—one of God's greatest inventions. We'll explain how he "wired" us, how the brain works, how it learns, and how each brain is unique.

THE PROCESS OF FARMING FAITH

Another fascinating overtone appears in the Parable of the Sower and other biblical agricultural metaphors. Jesus chooses farming to illustrate the seeding, germination, growth, and fruit-bearing of a believer's faith. Notice the deliberate choice of the metaphor. Farming is a process. It's a process consisting of certain steps and seasons— steps and seasons that any good farmer can learn.

We live in an age when this lesson needs to be learned. Most attempts at Christian education today concentrate almost exclusively on the content and not the process. Church leaders grumble about biblically illiterate congregations. But who's to blame? Perhaps all the attention has been directed at the content (the seeds), and none to the process (how seeds are successfully received, nurtured, and reproduced). Case in point: Our research shows most churches choose their Sunday school curriculum solely on content. "What does it cover?" they ask. Very few also ask, "How does it cover the material? What's the process for learning?"

Bud knows about process. Farming—transforming seeds into mature crops—is a process. The harvest doesn't just pop into the barn. Farming follows a fairly predictable sequence of events.

Learning about God, committing to follow Christ, growing in faith, and bearing fruit are events that form a process of faith development. The more we understand the process the better we'll be at farming faith.

But we'll never understand it completely. Part of the process is beyond our control and entirely miraculous. Even Bud admits this. He can tell you a lot about successful farming. But he simply cannot explain how that little corn seed knows how to re-create itself into a seven-foot tall green plant that bears a finished product of neatly lined up rows of succulent corn kernels. "That," he says, "is simply a miracle. And I get to witness it every year."

We, too, witness a miracle every year when we see our people grow in their faith and bear fruit. As God's servants we do our part. But we leave the heart of the process up to him. The Apostle Paul says it well in 1 Corinthians 3:6-7:

> "I planted the seed, Apollos watered it, but God made it grow. So neither he who plants nor he who waters is anything, but only God, who makes things grow."

AUTHENTIC LEARNING

We've developed a process approach to learning in the church that we call "authentic learning." We've chosen that term carefully.

"Authentic" means real. "Authentic learning" means learning that works. And, to our way of thinking, learning is not real—it does not really work—until learners understand, retain the learning, apply the learning to their lives, and bear fruit. This is Parable-of-the-Sower kind of learning.

Over the years we've collected a barnful of authentic learning approaches that really work, that really bear fruit. We've incorporated them into the curriculum and other educational materials we produce at Group Publishing. And we shared some of them in our earlier book, *Why Nobody Learns Much of Anything at Church: And How to Fix It*. Since then, people have asked us to gather and share more insights with them.

The Dirt on Learning looks at learning within the framework of the Parable of the Sower. We'll examine the hard-packed road—why some hear but they don't understand. We'll investigate the rocky ground—why some hear but they quickly forget. We'll explore some thorny weeds—how worries and temptations kill the learning process. And we'll find out how your efforts can bear fruit in the lives you touch.

"I touch the future. I teach."

Christa McAuliffe

Falling Along the Path

"A farmer went out to sow his seed.
As he was scattering the seed, some fell along
the path, and the birds came and ate it up.

When anyone hears the message about the kingdom and
does not understand it,
the evil one comes and snatches away
what was sown in his heart.
This is the seed sown along the path."

MATTHEW 13:3-4, 19

Don't just breeze by this familiar passage. It's loaded with implications for anyone who wishes to spread the good news.

In Jesus' day the fields were crisscrossed with footpaths. No fences held back the travelers. Over time, as traffic increased, the paths became trodden and hard packed. What once were ribbons of fertile soil became ridges of barren land. Any seeds that fell upon the crusty paths were doomed. The quality of the seed did not matter. The amount of rainfall was inconsequential. The seeds cast upon the paths were doomed.

The seeds could not snuggle into the earth because the packed topsoil barred their entry. They could only flounder atop the ground until hungry birds swooped to gobble them up. These seeds would never produce fruit. They had no chance to even sprout.

What is the core problem that Jesus presents in this metaphor? Is it the presence of the birds—identified by Jesus as the evil one? No, it seems the birds are a given, an undeniable reality of farming.

Still to this day, farmers like Bud are bothered from time to time by birds. But Bud knows that problem is not going away. He cannot rid South Dakota of hungry birds. No matter what he tries, the birds will always be around. They will always come to snatch what is easily snatched.

The problem is not the birds. The problem is not the evil one.

The problem here is the lack of understanding. Jesus is telling us directly that without understanding, his word will not stick. Yet how much teaching seed that is scattered into the pews and classrooms of today's churches is never understood? You see, the question is not, "What shall we do about the evil one?" The question is, "How can we sow in such a way that our people truly understand?"

THE CHANGING SOIL

Before we dig into practical application, we ask you to consider another intriguing facet of this metaphor. Before the ground was trodden into hard-packed paths, it was likely fertile and fruit-bearing. But circumstances changed. Soil that once worked for the sower no longer bore fruit.

Bud knows this phenomenon. For fifty years he's been adapting to shifting field conditions, equipment modifications, and new agricultural knowledge. Some things that once worked no longer work today. Bud has not continued to be successful by stubbornly clinging to the farming methods of yesteryear.

Bud has witnessed firsthand the disappearance of family farms in America. It seems every month or so another nearby farmer takes out an ad in the newspaper for an auction sale. Bud attends some of these bittersweet events. Sometimes he's the successful bidder on equipment he needs. But he knows it's equipment the seller can no longer afford. The auction is an eerie sort of wake for a family farm that's gasping its last breaths. When the auctioneer shouts that final "sold!" it means another small American farm has withered and died. A victim of changing times.

But Bud has been a student of those changing times. He's changed how he sows.

Can we do the same? We know God and his Word are unchanging. But how we sow his seeds must adapt to the ever-changing fields in which God has placed us.

The chapters that follow may challenge you to change how you approach teaching and learning. This is not a condemnation of how you've sown seed in the past. How people taught and learned in the past is like how people farmed fifty years ago. What may have produced acceptable results in the past may not bring the necessary harvest today.

It's time to trade in the old tractor. It's time to try a new fertilizer. It's time to change.

"When evening comes, you say,
'It will be fair weather, for the sky is red,'
and in the morning,
'Today it will be stormy, for the sky is red and overcast.'
You know how to interpret the appearance of the sky,
but you cannot interpret the signs of the times."

MATTHEW 16:2-3

CHAPTER TWO

GOOD CONTENT, POOR UNDERSTANDING

*"We have a lot of evidence that teaching content alone,
and hoping it will cause students to learn to think, doesn't work.
The teaching of content alone is not enough."*

ARTHUR COSTA

The eager second-graders crowded around their Sunday school teacher. She unfurled her creativity on these kids for forty-five minutes. She earnestly tried to cement into these young minds a line from 1 Samuel 16:7—"The Lord looks at the heart."

She repeated the verse over and over. She led a creative craft time, allowing each child to build little finger rings with reminder clues from the verse. She directed the kids to repeatedly sing the verse along with prerecorded music. It was a multi-sensory Lord-looks-at-the-heart barrage for forty-five minutes.

After observing this colorful session, we were curious about the students' response to the lesson. What had they learned? We questioned them immediately upon the conclusion of the class. "What was your lesson about today?" we asked. What we heard was enough to discourage even the cheeriest optimist.

Some couldn't remember a single thing. Most could not repeat the passage word for word. Some remembered the Scripture reference. "First Samuel 16:7," they'd spout in answer to our question. To those we'd ask, "What was that about?" They were generally clueless or gave vague, hollow answers.

One boy nearly reduced us to tears. He had participated in the class along with the other students. He had listened to the teacher read the verse. He had made the rings. He had sung the "Lord looks at the heart" song, over and over. And when he emerged from the classroom, we asked, "What was your lesson about today?"

He said, "Umm, I'm trying to remember. It was John 3:16." That verse was never taught, read, mentioned, or referred to in any way that Sunday.

"OK," we said, "what is that verse?"

"Whoever believes in God shall not perish but have everlasting life," he said rather haltingly.

"What does that mean?" we asked.

"That if you perish God you'll go to heaven," he said.

"What does perish mean?" we asked.

"To praise him."

When Understanding Is Forgotten

What a sad indictment.

That teacher scattered seeds along the path. The seeds were good. Her lesson never wavered from the Word of God. She worked hard to infuse her creativity into the lesson. She wrote the Scripture on a poster. She repeated the verse over and over. She taught the kids to make reminder rings. She led them in song. This was a hard-working teacher who loved those kids. She dearly wanted to "hide the Word" in their hearts.

What went wrong? How could the good seed so quickly become mere birdseed? The Parable of the Sower supplies the answer.

"When anyone hears the message about the kingdom and does not understand it, the evil one comes and snatches away what was sown in his heart" (Matthew 13:19a).

Understanding is the key. Without understanding, the seed—though perfect in every respect—falls along the hard-packed path. There it sits briefly on the surface until it is snatched away.

This teacher, with all good intentions, creatively cast those seeds upon the path. But she overlooked one crucial factor—understanding. Though her presentation of the verse was creative and varied, she spent practically no time exploring the meaning of the passage. To the children the verse was merely a collection of forgettable words.

CATALOGING THE CONTENT

How could the teacher overlook what seems so obvious? Sadly, this happens all the time. To one degree or another, we've all been lulled into believing that content alone is the focus. We've all grown up in an educational system that has elevated mere facts to idol status. Since first grade we've been drilled on the facts:

"What are the primary colors?"

"What's the capital of Rhode Island?"

"What is water made of?"

"When was the Great Depression?"

Our teachers demonstrated over and over that memorization of facts was the whole idea behind school. That was obviously what was most important. After all, we were tested on the dates of the Great Depression. We were not asked why it happened or what significance it might have for people today. If we wanted to pass the test we needed to know the "what"—not the "why." The "why," we learned, was simply not important.

The most "successful" students were those who could mentally catalog thousands of largely irrelevant facts. They went on to become the valedictorians, the schools' most exemplary success stories.

But what is success? Is it truly the ability to temporarily retain multitudes of miscellaneous facts? That may earn good grades. But is that the real goal of education? Consider the findings of an ongoing study of eighty-one valedictorians and salutatorians from the class of 1981 in Illinois high schools. These top students continued to achieve well in college. But by their late twenties most had found only average success in their chosen professions. Only one in four had kept pace with others of comparable age in higher levels of success. Many were doing much poorer than the average.

Karen Arnold, one of the researchers tracking these valedictorians, said, "I think we've discovered the 'dutiful'—people who know how to achieve in the system...To know that a person is a valedictorian is to know only that he or she is exceedingly good at achievement as measured by grades. It tells you nothing about how they react to the vicissitudes of life."[1]

> *"Learning without wisdom*
> *is a load of books on a donkey's back."*
> Zora Neale Hurston

SNATCHING WHAT'S SOWN IN THE HEART

It's a myth that most people find success and fulfillment through mere knowledge of facts. But the myth is alive and writhing in the church. That's what derailed that second-grade Sunday school class. The teacher believed the children's mere knowledge of the verse from 1 Samuel would deliver success. But not only did the children fail to remember the verse, they never caught its meaning or its relevance to their lives.

Even if the kids had been able to repeat the verse, without the critical element of understanding they were destined to come up empty-handed. It's the Parable of the Sower: If a learner doesn't understand the message, "the evil one comes and snatches away what was sown in his heart."

It's interesting that Jesus chose the "heart" imagery in this parable. It so happens this is the same imagery used in Psalm 119:11a:

"I have hidden your word in my heart."

Children's ministry workers who promote extensive Bible memory drills often quote this verse to support their efforts. But Jesus' teaching in the Parable of the Sower zeroes in on those who attempt to sow in the heart without developing real understanding. When people don't understand what's sown in their hearts, they're vulnerable. They're like hard-packed soil along the path. The seeds simply will not take root.

In our book *Why Nobody Learns Much of Anything at Church: And How to Fix It*, we explored how the memorization of Bible words and facts has itself become the goal in some churches.[2] Elaborate programs have been built around casting seeds on the hard-packed path. Children are rewarded with badges, trinkets, and candy for parroting bits of Scripture. (We'll examine the danger of those rewards later in this book.) But what is the result? The Parable of the Sower lays it out for us: Without understanding, the seed will never produce fruit. Jesus is calling us to produce more than birdseed.

So how can we avoid casting seeds upon the path? Let's look at a few practical guidelines.

1. Focus learning on understanding.

Our son Matt loves the water. As a matter of fact, he loved the water before he knew how to swim. In those younger years, he wore little inflatable devices on his arms to keep him afloat. With carefree abandon he'd leap into pools, lakes, and oceans. The little inflatable rings would keep his giggling head above water.

We told Matt he needed to wear the arm floaties whenever he wanted to swim. We taught him their name—Schwimminfluegels. We showed him how to put them on. But something was missing in our safety training.

One day, four-year-old Matt rushed to the pool in a community center and jumped in at the deep end—without his Schwimminfluegels! He promptly sank to the bottom. Thankfully we were near enough to jump in and pull him out before he had a chance to ingest much of the pool's water.

"Matt, why didn't you wear your Schwimminfluegels?" we asked.

"I just wanted to wear my swimming suit this time," he said.

He thought the arm floaties were merely optional apparel, like his swimsuit! He didn't understand how they worked. He didn't connect that those devices kept his head above water. We realized we'd told him some facts about the Schwimminfluegels, but we'd failed to explain how they worked to save his life in the water. He'd never understood what would happen if he would jump in without them. He'd never really grasped *why* he needed them.

Understanding is essential to learning and to applying learning to real life. Facts are often helpful. But understanding is crucial.

Jesus knew this well. Examine his teaching. How often did he drill his followers on facts? Rarely. Instead Jesus emphasized *understanding* of spiritual truths. Look at the Parable of the Sower. Jesus told the story to help his followers *understand* what he meant about the importance of teaching for *understanding!*

Jesus always taught with a clear goal in mind. What was his teaching goal? Obviously it was not mere transfer of facts. Michael D. Warden, in his book *Extraordinary Results From Ordinary Teachers*, writes that Jesus' teaching goal is summed up in John 17:1b-8:

> Father, the time has come. Glorify your Son, that your Son may glorify you. For you granted him authority over all people that he might give eternal life to all those you have given him. Now this is eternal life: that they may know you, the only true God, and Jesus Christ, whom you have sent. I have brought you glory on earth by completing the work you gave me to do. And now, Father, glorify me in your presence with the glory I had with you before the world began. I have revealed you to those whom you gave me out of the world. They were yours; you gave them to me and they have obeyed your word. Now they know that everything you have given me comes from you. For I gave them the words you gave me and they accepted them. They knew with certainty that I came from you, and they believed that you sent me.

From this, Warden concludes that Jesus came to give people a way to know God intimately. Warden writes:

> "The ultimate goal of Christian teaching is to draw people into a genuine, personal relationship with God."[3]

This is a worthy goal. But do you suppose mere transferring of Bible facts will likely lead to that goal's accomplishment? It's not likely. That's why Jesus spent his time emphasizing understanding, not mere fact-sowing.

Facts and Assessment

Why has the practice of fact-transferal become so prominent in education today—both Christian and secular? One likely reason pops to the surface. Fact knowledge is easy to assess. Consider most school tests. They're largely fact-based multiple-choice, true/false, fill-in-the-blank affairs that are easy to grade. But, sadly, what's easy to grade is often of lesser importance.

In the church we've emulated the public school model. As teachers we gauge children's Christian education progress by their readiness to answer factual questions such as, "Where was Jesus born?" We evaluate adults' proficiency by their ability to answer questions such as, "Which are the synoptic Gospels?" Churches have typically structured assessments of learning around mere facts. And, predictably, teachers and students tend to focus on what gets evaluated. Understanding, because it's harder to evaluate, gets left behind.

We've missed the point. But we're not alone. Christ's followers have been missing the point for centuries. That's why we need the Parable of the Sower.

"Much learning does not teach understanding."
Heraclitus

An Experience of Understanding

How does a lesson look when understanding is the focus? Let's look at Ephesians 4:29: "Do not let any unwholesome talk come out of your mouths, but only what is helpful for building others up according to their needs, that it may benefit those who listen." We like to use this verse with teenagers. But we don't merely read the verse. We don't insist the teenagers memorize the verse. We don't ask them to fill out a worksheet on the verse. We don't preach at them about the verse. We don't quiz them about who wrote the verse.

We strive for understanding and application of this verse. Here's how. We place the students in small groups and give each group a paper doll. We ask that each person take the doll and think of a common verbal put-down. Then they say that nasty word or phrase as they tear off an arm or leg or head of the doll. After a few minutes, the doll is reduced to scraps, and the air is filled with unkind words.

Then we read the verse and ask the students to think of kind words that build people up as mentioned in the verse. As they say those words, they're urged to tape the paper doll back together. Often the dolls have been so mutilated the students find it impossible to patch them together again.

We conclude by asking the groups to discuss a series of questions such as, "Which was easier for you, tearing the doll apart or putting it back together? How is this like real life? In light of the Scripture passage, who is someone who needs to hear a kind word from you this week? How will you tell them?" The students make profound discoveries. These simple paper dolls become highly memorable visual and tactile symbols of the verbal victims everybody knows.

After this simple but powerful experience, students understand the meaning of this verse. The seeds fall on fertile soil. They take root. They bear fruit.

Neither Mere Creativity nor Mere Facts

Now we must express a cautionary note here. Please don't misunderstand the essence of the previous example. The paper doll experience works. But it works not because it's a creative activity. It works because it achieves student understanding of the biblical principle.

Our educational goal is not to be merely creative. The second-grade teacher cited at the beginning of this chapter used very creative activities that related to 1 Samuel 16:7. But her students did not understand. They did not learn.

At Group Publishing, we've been creating educational materials for the church for twenty-five years. We're thankful that our curriculum is being used in more and more churches. People tell us it's "very creative." But that's not the point. Lots of materials look creative. Unless they result in deep understanding and application of biblical truths, the creativity amounts to only a "clanging gong."

Lynda Freeman is a Michigan-based Christian education specialist who consults with churches. She reports that church leaders often select curricular materials because they contain creative-looking activities. "But so often those activities simply focus on Bible facts, not on understanding or application," she said. "Students might learn the facts but not know how to live."

Creativity is not the goal. Creative activities can (and should) be used, but each should add to students' understanding and application of biblical truths. If your curriculum is creative but seems to focus merely on facts, it's time to reread the Parable of the Sower.

Some Christian educators say that children's curriculum should concentrate wholly on the acquisition of Bible facts. "Understanding and application can come later," they say. We wonder what Jesus would say about that. Look at his quote in Matthew 18:3:

"I tell you the truth, unless you change and become like little children, you will never enter the kingdom of heaven."

What childlike characteristics are we to emulate? A mind full of facts? Or a humble understanding that leads to trust and faith?

Depositing Bible facts in students' minds can be useful and helpful. Factual knowledge can aid the process of understanding. But our students—of any age—need to plainly see that factual knowledge is not the goal. Jesus came to live and die for us not so that we become walking encyclopedias of data, but faithful followers committed to a loving relationship with him.

> *"My heart is singing for joy this morning.*
> *A miracle has happened!*
> *The light of understanding has shone*
> *upon my little pupil's mind,*
> *and, behold, all things are changed!"*
>
> ANNIE SULLIVAN, HELEN KELLER'S TEACHER

2. Don't obscure understanding with puzzles.

Jesus surely had a long-term sense of time during his earthly ministry. His teachings were intended not only for those living at the time, but for the many generations yet to come. We suspect he clearly saw our current generation when he spoke the Parable of the Sower. We surmise this because we can think of no more glaring example of seed being hopelessly cast on the path than the current proliferation of student worksheets.

We're referring to those Sunday school papers that dominate most brands of curriculum. From preschool through adult, they take the form of crossword puzzles, word scrambles, mazes, word searches, fill-in-the-blanks, and rebuses. The creators of this material believe they're adding interest to the Scriptures. But we contend they're adding confusion, wasting time, and blocking understanding.

Here's an example of an upper-elementary worksheet exercise in a popular curriculum from a denominational publishing house.

MEMORY VERSE SCRAMBLE

Can you read the verse? Each letter in the verse should be the letter after it in the alphabet (b=c, z=a and so forth).

S Q T R S   H M S G D   K N Q C

Z M C   C N   F N N C   Psalm 37:3

What is the value of this exercise? How is this preferable to simply reading the verse in an actual Bible? Does this exercise illuminate and clarify the passage for the child? Does it enhance understanding? Is it the best possible use of time?

On the next page is another example. This one comes from a well-known nondenominational publisher.

WHO HAS TOLD YOU ABOUT JESUS?

Look in the maze of letters to find the names of people who might have told you about Jesus.

Draw a line through the letters that make a name. (Look for: MOTHER, FATHER, AUNT, UNCLE, GRANDMA, GRANDPA, TEACHER, MINISTER, SISTER, BROTHER, NEIGHBOR, FRIEND.)

"Mother" is done for you.

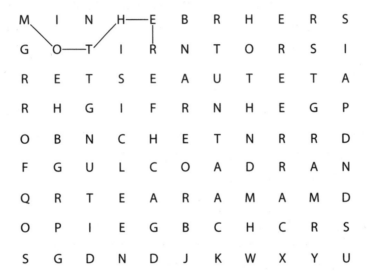

How will students grow closer to God as a result of this exercise? What new insight is gained? How is understanding enhanced?

Keep in mind that such worksheet exercises are not isolated examples. They are common to most publishers' student worksheets. We sometimes show examples like these in our Christian education workshops. Teachers howl in laughter. But they admit they still use them—week in and week out. Why?

Can you imagine Jesus teaching with such devices? Can you

picture him using these to teach the Parable of the Sower? "OK, people, see if you can figure out where the first seed fell. I've scratched some letters in the dirt here. Just unscramble these letters and you'll find the answer. Ready? Go!"

We've pledged we'll never include such exercises in the curriculum we create. Why? Because we know they do not help students understand and apply God's Word. In fact they can cloud and obscure understanding. Quite simply, they don't work. If they did, we'd all be using similar approaches in training situations elsewhere in life. We'd be using word puzzles to train computer operators. We'd be using mazes to train restaurant cooks. We'd be using crossword puzzles to train airline pilots. But these worksheets don't work.

If you find such time-wasting birdseed in your church's curriculum, it's time to reread the Parable of the Sower. And it's time to switch to a new curriculum that helps your learners genuinely understand the meaning of God's Word.

3. Use plain language.

Remember the second-grade boy's explanation of John 3:16? He thought "perish" was the same as "praise." His understanding of this fundamental verse was convoluted because the vocabulary was unfamiliar to him.

How often does this happen? How often do we cast word-seeds that we assume are growing as intended in fertile minds? It happens all too often. Seed falls upon the hard-packed path when we use words our learners do not clearly understand.

Let's look at a simulation of a Bible verse as it might sound to a child who is unfamiliar with some of the words. We've replaced those words with gobbledygook.

"Since we have now been pleebahed by his zicker, how much more shall we be chinged from Woo's bap through him! For if, when we were Woo's sathers, we were dumpneyed to him through the death of his laklak, how much more, having been dumpneyed, shall we be chinged through his life! Not only is this so, but we also goosh in Woo through our Ted-Smed-Ked, through whom we have now received dumpneyation."

To this child, what's the message? What hope could we have of these seeds sprouting? This example seems silly, but next Sunday thousands of children will be confounded by language they hear in church.

What was this verse? It was actually Romans 5:9-11. Let's look at it in the New International Version. Can you see how a child (or many adults, for that matter) might stumble over some of these words?

"Since we have now been justified by his blood, how much more shall we be saved from God's wrath through him! For if, when we were God's enemies, we were reconciled to him through the death of his Son, how much more, having been reconciled, shall we be saved through his life! Not only is this so, but we also rejoice in God through our Lord Jesus Christ, through whom we have now received reconciliation."

We have nothing against the NIV or against any other solid modern translation. But if our people do not understand our terminology, we are casting seeds upon the path. The lack of understanding will prevent the seeds from taking root.

When teaching God's Word to children, we can take two simple steps. First, select a Bible translation with a lower reading level, one that uses simpler, more understandable words. Then, always take time to explain all Bible passages, taking special care to clarify the meaning of the words.

Words That Cause Adults to Stumble

This advice goes for youth and adult audiences as well. All too often we use words that sail over the heads of grown-ups. We assume vocabulary knowledge where none exists. And with adults this problem can go undetected forever. At least with children, they'll often tell you if they don't understand a word or concept. But adults are usually too embarrassed to admit they don't know the meaning of a word. They fear admission would signal to others that they lack intelligence or sophistication. So they nod politely as they listen to what sounds to them like gobbledygook.

When you speak or write to adults in your congregation, are you certain they understand the meaning of the words you routinely use? We decided to quiz typical churchgoing adults on a list of "churchy" words, just to see how they'd define them. We surveyed a cross section of adults who are active members of churches of various denominations. Take a look at some of their definitions:

SANCTIFICATION:

"praise in groups"
"salvation"

RAPTURE:

"wrath"
"singing and dancing"
"broken heart"
"beginning"

EPIPHANY:

"greatness"
"gift certificate"
"church outlook"
"Catholics who celebrate Christmas"
"a short symphony"

ABSOLUTION:	ANOINTED:
"a mathematical term"	"being baptized"
"positive all the way"	"to be a king"
PARISH:	**NARTHEX:**
"where the preacher lives"	"chemical warfare"
"someone who's gone to hell"	"a small hole in the ground that worms live in"

Wow! How often do we believe we're really communicating when in fact we're infecting the congregation with confusion? We've walked into churches where the preacher and the teachers droned on for hours with churchy language that surely left many people more confused than when they entered. What possibly can be gained by this? Why not use simple terms that are understood by everyone, especially by the uninitiated?

Notice the communication style of Jesus. He never tried to impress others by using lofty words. He spoke plainly. He used common terms that connected with common people. He sowed seed that took root and bore fruit.

4. Use good questions to deepen understanding.

In an educational setting, questions can be powerful teaching tools. But poor questions can chew up valuable time and delay understanding.

Church teachers and leaders can ask quality questions that cause people to think and enrich their understanding. But, sadly, most teachers and leaders use questions merely to check students' knowledge of facts. That's casting seeds on the path.

Jesus modeled great question-asking for us. He asked lots of questions. More than two hundred are recorded in the Gospels. But very few of his questions were used to quiz listeners about facts. Roy B. Zuck writes in *Teaching as Jesus Taught:*

> Seldom did Jesus ask recall questions, merely asking for a recital of facts. If he did ask a "What-do-you-remember" question, it was to lead on to interaction on an important issue. More often he challenged his students with "What-do-you-think?" questions. The disciples never had to guess at an answer, trying to discover what he had in mind. Instead, they were encouraged to think for themselves, to offer their own opinions and ideas.[4]

Jesus asked great questions, the kind that encouraged thinking and pushed for understanding. Let's look at a few:

"If the salt loses its saltiness, how can it be made salty again?" (Matthew 5:13).

"Which is lawful on the Sabbath: to do good or to do evil, to save life or to kill?" (Mark 3:4).

"If you do good to those who are good to you, what credit is that to you?" (Luke 6:33).

Unfortunately, questions such as these are rarely asked at church. Instead time is often squandered on fact-finding questions such as: What were Noah's sons' names? Where was Jesus born? Where was Paul converted? What's worse, these types of questions are typically asked in classroom settings. The teacher asks a fact-finding question, and one student typically supplies the answer. The rest of the class sits passively.

PROBLEMS WITH FACT-FINDING QUESTIONS

Why is this done? For three basic reasons, we believe. While teacher intentions are good, none of these reasons is justified.

First, teachers often realize the Bible story or concept requires basic student familiarity with the facts. So, in an effort to make the facts known, the teacher asks a fact-based question. But why? The question format is usually not the clearest, most expedient, or most powerful method to convey facts. If facts are needed, teachers can usually be more effective by telling a story, showing a picture, acting out the concept, or engaging all students in fact-finding missions. Why leave fact delivery up to unprepared students? Class time is usually made even worse because students often have to sit through umpteen "wrong" answers before the teacher hears the "right" answer he or she is seeking. Why waste the time? If facts need to be made known, make them known in a memorable way and move on.

Second, well-intentioned teachers attempt to use fact-finding questions to break up a lecture and involve the students. But these types of questions generally have one right answer the teacher is seeking. So, necessarily, that means one student with the one correct answer gets to interact with the teacher. The other students are either discouraged for giving wrong answers or they simply sit passively while Smarty-pants gives the answer the teacher is looking for. That's not quality student interaction.

Third, teachers often ask fact-based questions as a form of assessment. They're trying to determine how much students know. But this is a very inefficient and unreliable form of assessment. If we stand before a class of twenty students and ask, "How big was Noah's ark?" what or who are we assessing? Typically one or two hands go up. Smarty-pants may supply the right answer. So what have we assessed? We've assessed that Smarty-pants knows the answer to this question. So what? What about the other nineteen? How do we know what they know? This kind of assessment is a waste of time.

The teacher behavior we've just described is not limited to teachers of children. We regularly see teachers of adults follow the same fruitless path. They'll read a Bible passage, and then ask the entire class or congregation a fact-recall question. For adult students this is not only tedious, it's usually insulting to their intelligence. So many times we've endured adult classes where the teacher asks a string of fact-recall questions. We've been tempted to say, "If you're looking for some fact you already know, spare us the routine. Just tell us. Then let us get on with understanding how this subject can bear fruit in our lives."

CHARACTERISTICS OF GOOD QUESTIONS

If we're concerned about those ill-cast seeds on the path, we need to ask questions that deepen understanding. Good educators sometimes refer to four characteristics of quality questions:[5]

1. **OPEN-ENDED.** These are questions that cannot be solved with a pat answer. They require students to think. The object is not to read the teacher's mind. Example: Jesus asked, "Why do you look at the speck of sawdust in your brother's eye and pay no attention to the plank in your own eye?" (Matthew 7:3).

2. **NONJUDGMENTAL.** There's no single right answer with this type of question. In order to answer, students need to search themselves. Example: Jesus asked, "Why are you troubled, and why do doubts rise in your minds?" (Luke 24:38).

3. **EMOTIVE AND INTELLECTUALLY STIMULATING.** These questions stir and challenge. They electrify students to grapple and seek understanding. Example: Jesus said, "If Satan drives out

Satan, he is divided against himself. How then can his kingdom stand? And if I drive out demons by Beelzebub, by whom do your people drive them out?" (Matthew 12:26-27a).

4. **SUCCINCT.** Great questions often contain only a handful of words, yet they demand a lot. Example: Jesus asked, "Why did you doubt?" (Matthew 14:31b).

Asking good questions is hard work. When we coach Christian curriculum writers, we challenge them to spend substantial blocks of their time devising great questions. The questions are at least as important as any other part of the lesson.

We can help people develop a fuller understanding of God's Word by asking good questions. As we increase understanding, we decrease the likelihood that our seeds will fall along the path where they'll be snatched by birds.

REFERENCES

1. The Chicago Tribune (May 29, 1992). Interview with Karen Arnold, professor of education at Boston University, who researched the valedictorians along with Terry Denny at the University of Illinois. Quoted by Daniel Goleman in *Emotional Intelligence* (New York, NY: Bantam Books, 1997), 35-36.

2. Thom and Joani Schultz, *Why Nobody Learns Much of Anything at Church: And How to Fix It* (Loveland, CO: Group Publishing, 1993), 61-77.

3. Michael D. Warden, *Extraordinary Results From Ordinary Teachers* (Loveland, CO: Group Publishing, 1998), 47-48.

4. Roy B. Zuck, *Teaching as Jesus Taught* (Grand Rapids, MI: Baker Books, 1995), 255.

5. Adapted from Rob Traver, "What Is a Good Guiding Question?" Educational Leadership, (March 1998), 71.

CHAPTER THREE

A LEARNER-BASED APPROACH

They call it the Parable of the Sower. But it really ought to be called the Parable of the Dirt. The story is not so much about the sower as it is about the various types of ground onto which the seed is cast.

Jesus' focus in this story is the dirt, the land of the learner. First he tells us about the hard-packed ground, then the rocky ground, then the thorny ground, and finally the good ground. Who gets the starring role in this story? The dirt!

Now, when we think about spreading God's Word among our people, for whom should we design our process? Those doing the teaching or those doing the learning? What's the desired result of Christian education? That God's Word is taught or that God's Word is learned?

The parable plainly illustrates that good seed can be vigorously spread yet still result in no fruit. The success of the crop depends upon the condition of the soil.

There's a profound lesson for us here. If our focus is merely on teachers and teaching, we'll produce little fruit. But if our focus shifts to the learner, it'll change everything we do.

For too long the church's focus has been confined to teaching. We propose it's time for a learner-based approach.

Colleges and universities are slowly coming to the same conclusion. The Denver Post reported in 1998 that Colorado State University President Al Yates said higher education is finally coming to grips with two truths:

"First, the fundamental product of the universityis not teaching, but learning. Second, the institution, not the student,must assume responsibility for the effectiveness of that learning."[1]

That's refreshing. Those two truths would make good educational principles for the church to consider also.

LEARNER-BASED CHARACTERISTICS

What do we mean by learner-based? It's an approach with a clear goal: that learners understand, retain, and apply their learning. The focus is on the learner, not the teacher. Its success is based not on how eloquently the sower casts seeds, but on whether the seeds take root and bear fruit. This shift of perspective is an enormous change for most churches. But the results are stunning—"yielding a hundred, sixty or thirty times what was sown" (Matthew 13:23b).

Let's look at some premises in the learner-based approach.

1. Learners are distinct and unique. People don't all learn the same way. Some learn primarily through their eyes, others through their ears, others through touch and movement. Some are analytical, others more random and global. Some learn faster than others. Learner-based strategies accommodate all learners.

2. What works for the learners is far more important than what's most comfortable for their teachers or leaders.

3. Learners help guide the learning process. They're allowed to make choices, follow their curiosity, and explore what interests them. They're encouraged to make learning relevant to their own lives.

4. Learning occurs best when learners enjoy the process. They'll learn and retain more when the curriculum brings delight; when friendships and interactions with other learners are encouraged; and when learners feel appreciated, respected and loved.

5. Education is evaluated on what learners understand, retain, and apply—not merely on what's taught, the completeness of the curriculum, or the eloquence of the teachers. Learning is effective when it creates learner appetite for more learning and an insatiable desire to share the learning with others.

A NEW PARADIGM FOR TEACHERS AND LEADERS

The learner-based approach requires a whole new mind-set for many church teachers and leaders. Let's compare a profile of a non-learner-based leader with that of a learner-based one.

A Non-Learner-Based Mind-Set

"My job is to teach. I'm successful when I cover the prescribed material for my students. I use our denominational Bible curriculum because it contains all the details of our doctrines. It's the same material I studied when I was a child. I know this material. And you know what they say, 'Good teachers always know more than their students.'

"I prefer to lecture for most of the hour, because I have so much good material to share. It's the only way to get through the curriculum. Besides, I feel I'm a good speaker. I'm comfortable in front of people. Myself, I like to listen to good speakers. I learn a lot from them.

"I run a pretty tight ship. I tell students they're here to learn. That means no fooling around. I expect them to sit still and listen to me. For students to respect me as a teacher, I must maintain my

role as the authority figure at all times. If students act up, I say, 'If you're not ready for serious Bible study, then you can just leave.' And some do. I've realized some students just don't want to learn."

A Learner-Based Mind-Set

"My job is to help students learn, grow, and apply biblical truths to their lives. I know I've been successful when I hear students relate how something they learned in class affected their lives during the week.

"We use a curriculum that really encourages students to get involved in the Bible lesson. They talk with one another and share their experiences that relate to the Bible story. When they share, I find I usually learn new insights myself!

"Our class isn't like anything I remember when I was in Sunday school. Some of these kids are really into art, so they depict the Bible story on the blackboard. Others are really musical, so they help lead the singing. Many of them really get into the simulation games we play. Nobody gets bored, that's for sure. And they really love being together.

"Sometimes our learning activities get a little loud. But it's because the kids are having so much fun! As long as they're learning and growing, I'll do my part to explain the noise to the rest of the congregation."

Do you see the difference? The first teacher is there to serve a system. The second is there to serve the students. The first tries to fit students into the teacher's mold. The second adapts the lesson, schedule, and environment to fit the students' needs, desires, and interests. The non-learner-based teacher attempts to teach from her own strengths. The learner-based teacher determines the students' strengths and then designs the class around them.

In the first example, discipline seems to be an ongoing problem. In the second example, students are too engaged to cause trouble. This is one of the byproducts of a learner-based approach. Discipline problems are much rarer.

Another byproduct is teacher enrichment and satisfaction. Notice how the learner-based teacher said, "I usually learn new insights myself!" That happens because the teacher isn't doing all the talking. Students are allowed and encouraged to contribute. And that enables the teacher to not only give but receive. Barbara L. McCombs and Jo Sue Whisler gathered considerable research in the field of learner-based education. In their book *The Learner-Centered Classroom and School,* they write: "We also found that teachers who are more learner centered are more successful in engaging more students in an effective learning process and are also more effective learners themselves and happier with their jobs."[2]

A STORY OF STUDENT RELEVANCE

The learner-based approach emphasizes linking the subject matter to students' real lives. Jesus was a master at this. His teachings were (and still are) always relevant. His words and actions had immediate application to the people around him.

Sandi Wright, a children's minister near Seattle, realized a new dimension of student relevance as she taught a lesson from Group Publishing's Hands-On Bible Curriculum™ to a class of sixth-graders. As a part of this experiential lesson, the kids were assigned various make-believe "disabilities," such as blindness and limb paralysis. Then they had to work together to help each other move across the room with their imagined disabilities. The kids really got into the experience, and a lively discussion followed. They felt new empathy for those with disabilities.

Sandi asked, "What disabilities do people your age have?" What she heard caught her off-guard. These kids listed "braces" as the number one disability affecting their peers. Instead of being teacher-based and discounting the kids' response, Sandi followed up. "How do braces affect people?" she asked. The students told her about pain, days missed from school, and the difficulty of tooth-brushing.

At that point in the lesson, the class stopped to pray for all who had braces on their teeth. The students—and the teacher—were deeply touched by a lesson that had an immediate relevance and life application. The kids learned about major disabilities such as blindness, but also applied their learning to a condition they encountered every day.

When we allow learners to help guide the learning process, they find avenues of relevance, ways to tie the Bible to their own lives.

BECOMING MORE LEARNER-BASED

Teachers and leaders can begin to understand and embrace the learner-based approach through some introspection. It's a natural tendency for teachers to teach in the way they were taught, or in the way they themselves most readily learn. How do you like to teach? Do you like to do most of the talking? Or do you like to engage students in small-group discussions? Do you like worksheets? Or do you prefer more active types of learning? Do you like to see students arranged at desks in neat rows? Or would you rather see them seated informally on the floor? Do you like being an authority figure? Or do you prefer being a helper and friend?

Now that you've thought about your own preferences, label them for what they are: TEACHER-BASED INCLINATIONS. Become aware of your leanings, your own biases. Now that these things are out in the open, you can move on to the next question: How can your students best learn? It's likely your students, at least many of them, do not share your preferences for learning. They did not grow up just like you. They do not have the same background, the same societal influences, the same brain makeup.

Be prepared to become a different kind of teacher, leader, or preacher. This new direction may be not be as comfortable as your old ways. But remember, being learner-based means doing what's best for the learner, not what's most comfortable for the teacher. Christ did not call us to follow him so that we would be comfortable. Quite the contrary, he warned that discipleship would be downright uncomfortable at times. "If anyone would come after me, he must deny himself and take up his cross and follow me," Jesus said in Matthew 16:24b.

So step out and reinvent yourself for the sake of your learners.

A New World of Learners

Leonard Sweet, seminary dean, author, church historian and futurist, writes in *Eleven Genetic Gateways to Spiritual Awakening:*

> It's time to stop talking about education and start talking about learning. Learning encompasses "anytime, anywhere, anybody, anything"... In fact...learning may be more central to a spiritual awakening than worship...We must free the church's educational system from the "lecture-drill-test" methods of the factory model. Religious learning systems must be based on new academic paradigms that shift from passive learning modes to active learning modes, especially ones where students learn habits of the mind and habits of the soul at their own rate and in their own area of special interest.[3]

Sweet says the church needs to understand that today's crop of learners is fundamentally different from previous generations. We've been shaped differently by the world around us. For example, he says our brains are being virtually "rewired." We're moving from being "linear" thinkers to "loopy" thinkers, he asserts.

Just look at popular television shows, Sweet says. Years ago *Bonanza* was the big hit. Every week it featured a very linear, very consecutive story line. The show opened with a situation, and gradually built, scene by scene, without detours, to the conclusion.

But then notice what happened to television shows by the time the '90s rolled around. What became the big hit? *ER*, the hospital drama. *ER* story lines are far from linear. They're "loopy." They loop in and out of different stories. They're layered, stacked, concurrent.

This show is a reflection of our society, Sweet says. People are learning in more loopy ways. They're navigating on the Internet, a medium that's really loopy—layered, stacked, concurrent. Today's kids are somehow able to watch TV, listen to music, talk on the phone, and do their homework—all at the same time!

The church's teacher-based model just doesn't work as well today. The learner-based approach calls us to observe how today's people are changing. They're becoming less linear, more random. Because of that, Sweet says, "I don't teach; I organize learning. I no longer write sermons; I create experiences."

LEARNER-BASED CURRICULUM

How should a church "organize for learning"? It begins by acknowledging that today's learners are different, and that each individual learns differently. For some time we've recognized that individuals possess different "learning styles." They learn more and retain it longer when the learning process taps into their individual styles.

Some people are more visually oriented. Others are more auditory. Some are more kinesthetic or tactile—they like to learn through touch and movement. We need to use fresh Christian learning materials that accommodate all learners' styles. The old, teacher-based stuff typically appeals to only one or two styles. It's laden with teacher talk and tedious worksheets. And it's typically very linear in approach—the lesson makes sense only if conducted in strict consecutive order. And the entire lesson must be covered to get to the conclusion.

We've been advocating Christian curriculum reform for some time. And we've been able to make available some products that are engineered to be learner-based. We're involved in the creation of Core Belief Bible Study Series for youth, Hands-On Bible Curriculum for children, and the FaithWeaver™ family of Christian growth resources.

All of these materials use an active, experiential approach— people learning by doing. It's a learner-based technique Jesus used. When Jesus wanted to teach a lesson of humble servanthood, he got down on his knees and washed his disciples' feet. He could have preached a sermon or handed out a worksheet. But he chose a method that he knew would really connect with those learners.

Some have said this active approach works with only one type of learner. We disagree. Just look at Jesus' example. The disciples who were more visually oriented *saw* a very memorable sight of the Messiah washing the men's dirty feet. The visual learners remembered the lesson. The auditory disciples *heard* their Lord's exchange with a defiant Peter. And they heard Jesus explain the significance of his act. The auditory learners remembered the lesson. The disciples who were more kinesthetically inclined *felt* Jesus take their feet and gently wash them clean. The touch/movement learners remembered the lesson.

So, you see, good active-learning experiences work with all types of learners. Active-learning curriculum is a wonderful solution for churches that wish to become more learner-based.

"What we have to learn to do,
we learn by doing."

ARISTOTLE

Another learner-based characteristic we've engineered into the curriculum we've created is what we call interactive learning. This is student-to-student talk. We've discovered people learn and retain more when they get to talk. By this, we're not referring to the typical setup where the teacher asks a question and one or two students respond to the teacher. True interactive learning enables *every* learner to talk—in pairs or small groups.

Some teachers avoid interactive learning because they believe student-to-student talk merely encourages the pooling of ignorance. This is a misunderstanding of the process. We use interactive learning not to transfer facts, but to enrich individual understanding. Interactive pairs and groups shouldn't be handed questions such as, "What were the three ways Peter denied Jesus?" Instead they might discuss questions such as, "Why do you suppose Peter denied Jesus?" and "What are ways we deny Christ in our everyday lives?" This type of interactive sharing does not "pool ignorance." Rather it encourages learners to understand and apply God's Word to their individual lives—in a way that teacher talk cannot.

Research has shown interactive learning results in deeper learning. But churches, teachers, and other curriculum publishers have been slow to incorporate it. Search Institute, a Minneapolis-based research organization, has undertaken extensive, significant studies of the effectiveness of Christian education. One such study examined education in the Lutheran Church—Missouri Synod (LCMS). Here's an excerpt from the research report:

> As important as educational content is an effective educational process. Among LCMS members, little correlation exists between faith maturity and leader-centered, one-way communication in Christian education (which can be called "passive learning"). That is to say that, in and of itself, knowledge imparted by a teacher has little impact on a person's growth in faith.
>
> By contrast, learning processes that engage people in interaction with the leader and with each other (which we term "interactive learning") have a significant impact on faith. In these settings, people talk about their understanding of God and help each other apply their faith to issues and concerns in their lives.
>
> Few youth or adults report frequently experiencing this kind of interactive educational environment...Only a quarter of adults and even fewer youth regularly experience an interactive educational process.
>
> This study asserts, then, that most congregations have not adopted an interactive learning style for youth or adult education. Instead, they continue to rely primarily on the transmission of information from a leader or speaker—a style that has less impact on people's faith.[4]

INTERACTIVE VS. PASSIVE LEARNING

Here are the percentages of adults and youth who reported these attributes of their church's Christian education in the Search Institute study of more than two thousand Lutherans. [5]

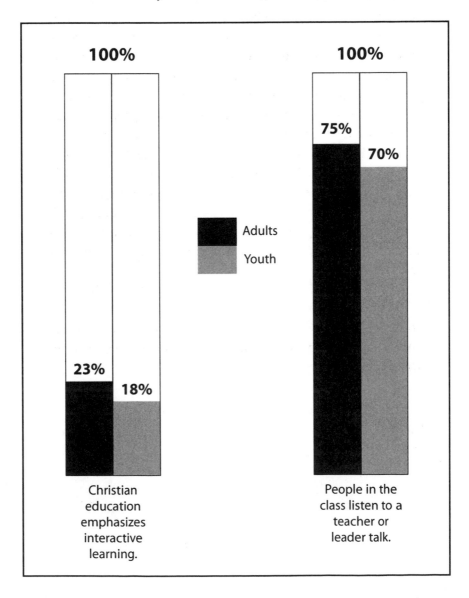

55

How would your church measure up in such a study? If you're ready to become more learner-based, perhaps it's time for a retooling of your curriculum. And it may be time for some focused teacher training. This book's companion teacher training kit will help get your teachers on board with authentic learning approaches.

> *"Get your students talking to each other,*
> *not just to you or to the air."*
>
> WAYNE C. BOOTH

DIFFERENT KINDS OF SMART

The learner-based approach assumes that all people can (and do) learn. They're all competent. They're all smart. But they're smart in different ways.

People used to talk a lot about IQ tests. These supplied educators with a single-number score that supposedly ranked a student relative to others according to intelligence. Many have taken issue with the thought that individual general intelligence can be so measured. Colin Rose and Malcolm J. Nicholl write in their book *Accelerated Learning for the 21st Century:*

> Intelligence tests measure the ability of people to do well in intelligence tests...Intelligence can vary by context. If you were stranded with an Aborigine in the middle of the Australian bush without food or water, she would be the intelligent one— because she would know how to survive. Transport her to your office and ask her to use your computer and the position would be reversed.[6]

Several years ago Harvard professor Howard Gardner questioned the value of the general intelligence construct. He proposed that people possess different kinds of intelligences. So far he's identified eight, and he's considering more.[7]

The theory of these eight intelligences has been useful to educators looking to understand how everyone learns differently. The theory is that each person has some combination of the intelligences. No one possesses exclusively just one intelligence. But everyone tends to dominate in one or two. We've supplied a brief description of each intelligence. We've also included some tips on how to help learners who seem to dominate in each of the intelligences. Use this information to help customize your teaching, to make your approach more learner-based.

Linguistic intelligence

Strengths: use of words—listening, reading, writing, speaking, memorizing
- Tell or read stories
- Use journal writing
- Engage students in discussion

Logical intelligence

Strengths: numbers, abstract thinking, logical reasoning, organization, problem solving
- Analyze and interpret what is studied
- Ask probing, thinking questions
- Involve students in problem solving

Visual-spatial intelligence

Strengths: art, drawing, imagination, use of metaphors
- Use pictures, posters, maps, and videos
- Let students doodle their understandings
- Plan arts and crafts activities

Musical intelligence

Strengths: music, rhythm, pitch, sensitivity to the emotional power of music
- Learn Bible truths through songs
- Encourage song writing
- Use music to set the mood

Bodily-kinesthetic intelligence

Strengths: athletics, dance, hand skills, acting
- Act out stories with drama and role-play
- Use physical movement, games, dance
- Have students build models of what they're studying

Intrapersonal intelligence

Strengths: understanding self, introspection, self-motivation, meditation
- Make time for quiet reflection
- Plan independent study times
- Debrief learning one-on-one

Interpersonal intelligence

Strengths: working with others, negotiation, awareness of others' needs
- Use interactive learning (pair shares, small groups)
- Do service projects
- Include mingling and get-acquainted time

Naturalist intelligence

Strengths: knowing, appreciating, and interacting with nature
- Conduct outdoor sessions
- Utilize plants, animals, and rocks in activities
- Emphasize God's creation of the universe

Christine Yount, editor of Children's Ministry Magazine, created a series of children's lessons that incorporate and accommodate these intelligences. She published them in the book *Forget-Me-Not Bible Story Activities.* Another book, *Making Scripture Memory Fun,* helps children learn God's Word through various experiences that use all eight intelligences.

And Group's new FaithWeaver Bible Curriculum also accommodates and provides emphases for learners with strengths in all types of intelligence.

CREATING A LEARNER-BASED ENVIRONMENT

How should your space be arranged to be most conducive for learning? Chairs arranged in neat rows? Probably not. That configuration is more fitting to the manufacturing mind-set of education—everybody gets the same treatment on a trudging assembly line.

Should chairs always face the teacher? Only if you're attempting to further the teacher-based mind-set that forces an authoritarian knowledge-dispenser image.

Do you need tables? Maybe not, unless you're still clinging to those old word puzzles.

Take time to think through what your learning environment says about your learning philosophy.

Leonard Sweet believes the church is moving from a content-driven institution to a relationship-driven organism. This relationship orientation returns the church to a Jesus style of ministry. Jesus was not so intent on teaching people religious content as he was on beckoning people into a genuine relationship with him and into compassionate relationships with one another. Do you like that philosophy? If so, how might that impact how you arrange your learning space? Does the space encourage relation-ships? Are seats arranged so that people easily meet others and feel comfortable sharing with one another?

A woman we'll call Helen volunteered to teach the crafts class at vacation Bible school. The director had set up the rooms. Be-cause of the nature of the crafts and the preferences of the chil-dren, no tables or chairs were placed in the crafts room. The kids loved it. The whole floor was their palette! But Helen hated it. "Why can't we have tables and chairs in here like a normal class-room?" she asked the director.

The director tried to explain that this setup was best for the children. But Helen insisted it was improper. Finally she admitted she didn't like sitting on the floor herself. (Aha! Another teacher-based infiltrator!) The director finally suggested Helen bring in her own chair, and the children could still spread out on the floor. That satisfied Helen.

Here's the good news. Helen ended the week praising the di-rector. "This was the best VBS! The children just loved it, and they got so much out of it! And I think they really liked using the whole floor for the art projects," she said, almost as if it were her idea all along.

That director took a learner-based approach to the learning environment. She resisted the temptation to cave in to the teacher-based desires of a grown-up. And the children benefited.

Arrange your space according to what most enhances your learners' experience. Don't hesitate to frequently change your con-figuration to suit the learning requirements of the moment.

GROUP STUDENTS FOR LEARNING

The teacher-based mind-set has traditionally grouped learners by age. This makes it convenient for teachers and leaders to organize and administrate. But is this always the best formula for the learners?

> *"Children are born when they're ready.*
> *They creep when they're ready.*
> *They teethe when they're ready.*
> *They walk when they're ready.*
> *They talk when they're ready.*
> *But they go to school, ready or not, when they're five."*
>
> JIM GRANT, EDUCATOR

Grouping learners strictly by age makes the assumption that everyone of a certain age develops at the same rate, learns at the same pace, has similar interests, and has identical needs. That's a faulty assumption. Same-age grading is an idea churches borrowed from the public schools. But even the schools are now rethinking this policy. Many are moving to multi-age classrooms—with considerable success.

Sometimes it makes sense to clump students together in mixed-age groupings. In this configuration, students learn and relate in the same way healthy families do. Families often contain children of varying ages. Somehow families share experiences in which all members enjoy them and learn from them. This idea can work with the family of God also.

Group Publishing's vacation Bible school programs recommend assembling kids of various ages into six-person learning teams. A team may have a student from each grade, kindergarten through fifth grade. These teams stay together throughout the VBS. And it works wonderfully! The directors and teachers report they find several advantages to these multi-age groups:

1. Enhanced learning. Students are able to move at their own pace. There's less pressure to keep up with peers. Older children often take time to tutor the younger ones, who love the extra attention. And it's good for the older students because they get to become "teachers." We all know who learns the most in any classroom. The teacher! So guess which kids really learn a lot!

2. Cooperation. Teachers report these mixed-age groups learn cooperation skills. They tend to help each other. The older ones look out for the younger ones. And the younger ones look up to the older ones.

3. Flexibility. Multi-aging works for any size church. If you have only a few kids, great! Put them together in one or two mixed-age groups. If you have hundreds of kids, great! Just assign them to as many mixed-age groups as you need. Facilities problems often go away too. You can evenly distribute students in the building without having to worry if you have too few first-graders or too many fourth-graders.

4. Discipline. This is a real blessing. Teachers have discovered that multi-aging eliminates discipline problems almost entirely. First you have the ability to split up those third-grade boys who always make trouble together. And the mixed ages tend to provide positive peer pressure to behave. The younger ones don't feel comfortable acting like goons in front of the older kids. And the older ones feel it's uncool to act immaturely around the little ones. It works!

The multi-age concept is a useful learner-based solution for many churches. It offers many benefits that have been forgotten since the days of the one-room schoolhouse. Joani attended one of those during her grade school days in South Dakota. She believes she learned more, developed deeper friendships, got more individual attention, and enjoyed the process more than she would have in a closely-graded school.

> *"Although humans are not usually born in litters,*
> *we seem to insist that they be educated in them."*
>
> LILLIAN KATZ,
> NATIONAL ASSOCIATION FOR THE EDUCATION OF YOUNG CHILDREN

REFERENCES

1. "CSU a good student," The Denver Post (May 11, 1998).

2. Barbara L. McCombs and Jo Sue Whisler, *The Learner-Centered Classroom and School* (San Francisco, CA: Jossey-Bass Inc., 1997), 24.

3. Leonard Sweet, *Eleven Genetic Gateways to Spiritual Awakening* (Nashville, TN: Abingdon Press, 1998), 44, 46.

4. Peter L. Benson, Eugene C. Roehlkepartain and I. Shelby Andress, *Congregations at Crossroads* (Minneapolis, MN: Search Institute, 1995), 19-20.

5. Benson, Roehlkepartain, and Andress, *Congregations at Crossroads,* 18-19.

6. Colin Rose and Malcolm J. Nicholl, *Accelerated Learning for the 21st Century* (New York, NY: Delacorte Press, 1997), 36-37.

7. Rose and Nicholl, *Accelerated Learning for the 21st Century,* 37-39.

Falling on Rocky Ground

"Some fell on rocky places,
where it did not have much soil.
It sprang up quickly, because the soil was shallow.
But when the sun came up, the plants were scorched,
and they withered because they had no root.

The one who received the seed that fell on rocky places
is the man who hears the word and at once receives it with joy.
But since he has no root, he lasts only a short time.
When trouble or persecution comes because of the word,
he quickly falls away."

Matthew 13:5-6, 20-21

Jesus' listeners could quickly connect with this message. They knew all about shallow soil and its danger to young plants.

Much of the soil in the Galilee area sits atop limestone bedrock. In some spots the layer of topsoil is shallow. There may be enough soil to surround a tender seed, and with some moisture the seed will sprout, poking its little green shoot into the warming sunshine. But there's not ample depth for the young root to anchor itself deeply. And without that depth, the root cannot tap into the deep life-giving water. Then the sun turns from warm friend to fiery foe, burning the little sprout to death.

Subterranean rocks in any farmer's field are bad news. But because they may not be immediately seen, they can fool a farmer into thinking everything's just fine. He casts his seeds, and in a short time they sprout. Looking good! But then the sprouts begin to wither and die. The farmer learns a hard lesson. Unless he deals with those unseen rocks, there'll be no harvest.

Bud knows all about rocks. Some fields he won't sow because he knows they're too rocky to support a crop. In all his other fields, he battles the rocks every year. In fact, his daughter Joani remembers clearly her childhood role in ridding the fields of rocks. She'd sit on the back of a flatbed wagon pulled by her dad's old tractor. When she or her dad would spot a rock, Joani would hop off, grab the stone, and toss it onto the wagon. This tedious routine would repeat over and over for hours and hours.

Joani hated picking up rocks. But it had to be done to make way for a successful crop. Bud owes some of his success today to Joani and other farmhands who freed the fields from rocks. The crops flourish today because their roots go deep.

Getting Your Hopes Up Too Soon

This part of Jesus' story holds some thought-provoking implications. He seems to indicate that we shouldn't assume our work is done after a person shows initial enthusiasm for the gospel. The parable's little plant "sprang up quickly," but it soon died. The man heard the word and received it with joy. But that's not what really matters.

Teachers and leaders often get all excited about someone's initial interest in the Lord. But it's discouraging to see that interest slip away after the luster vanishes.

What might we learn here about certain methods of evangelism? We wonder about evangelists who really know how to fire up a crowd. They make passionate and repeated invitations for people to "come forward." Throngs of people may huddle around the preachers and "receive the word with joy." At that moment they're excited. But then what happens? If no accommodation is made for their roots to reach down deeply, their interest in the Lord is likely to wither.

Jesus, through this parable, is warning us about shallowness. If the word is not deeply planted, it will not grow and produce fruit. The moment there's trouble or persecution our people may "quickly fall away."

If we're serious about sowing God's Word, we need to

be serious about implementing ways that cause the Word to take root. Jesus isn't interested in our efforts that cause a temporary sprout. We accomplish little when we drill learners on Bible material, only to see them forget the Word when the going gets tough. We need to find reliable ways to help people authentically learn, retain their learning long-term, apply that learning, and bear fruit.

Let's pick up a shovel and start digging—deeply.

CHAPTER FOUR

MOVING MEMORY FROM SHORT-TERM TO LONG-TERM

*I*s learning taking root among our people? To answer that question, we often like to go right to the source—the learners—and simply ask them.

We've visited many churches with extensive children's Scripture memory programs. We've spent many hours interviewing the children, asking them to tell us what they've learned, what they could remember. Many of the kids could repeat the Bible passage they had memorized for the day we visited. But very, very few could recite any other passages they'd been required to learn over recent weeks and months.

Here's how one interview went with a boy whose shirt was festooned with memory-achievement pins and badges.

> *Thom:* It looks like you really work hard to get all of these verses memorized. Why do you work so hard?
>
> *Boy:* So I can know them.
>
> *Thom:* What happens if you know them well?
>
> *Boy:* Then you get passed on here, and you can remember 'em most of your life.
>
> *Thom:* Good. Can you remember the one you learned for last week?
>
> *Boy:* Last week? Let's see. Umm, I don't think so.
>
> *Thom:* Two weeks ago?
>
> *Boy:* No, I don't think so.

Thom: How about the time before that?
Boy: Whoa! No way!
Thom: So do you remember any of them except this week's?
Boy: No, not really. Because I don't really look at them again.
              I look at a new verse so I can get that one.

We have hours and hours of taped interviews similar to this one. This boy's response, unfortunately, is not the exception. It's the norm.

What is the church doing? After untold hours of memory drilling, intricate programming, investment in reward badges and ribbons, what do we have to show for all of this? The Parable of the Sower may give us the stark answer:

"But since they have no root, they last only a short time" (Mark 4:17a).

Like a naive farmer, we sometimes sit back and proudly count all the little sprouts that appear in children's Scripture memory programs. But are temporary sprouts the goal? Is it enough that a seed briefly sprouts—only to wither and die within hours or days? Could it be that we're simply fooling ourselves—like a sower who casts his seed on rocky ground?

Adults and Sermons

Are children the only learners in the church who suffer from short-term memory loss? No, in fact they usually do better than older learners.

We polled adult churchgoers about what they remembered from recent sermons. On a Wednesday we asked adults from many different churches what they could recall about the previous weekend's sermon. Some could remember the general topic. A few could remember a point or two. But the overwhelming majority could not remember a single thing! Their memories were stripped clean of everything the preacher had said just a few days earlier.

Now, don't assume we interviewed only people who listen to boring preachers. These adults simply experienced what was quite a normal loss of memory. Research shows that 40 percent of a spoken message is lost from a listener's memory after just two minutes. After a half day, 60 percent of the message is gone. And after a week, over 90 percent of the message has leaked out of the memory forever.

How do today's preachers perceive themselves? How well do they believe their messages are sticking? Do they ever check the retention of their listeners a week later? What do they believe the Parable of the Sower has to say about people's retention of sermons? Would they preach any differently if they knew how to move a message from people's short- to long-term memory?

"Woe to him who teaches men faster than they can learn."

WILL DURANT

SCHOOLS AND SHORT-TERM MEMORY

Is the church the only institution suffering from short-term memory problems? Hardly. Our public schools have built entire systems around the temporary accumulation of information. Schools spend thousands upon thousands of hours drilling students on the names of all the presidents, state capitals, elements on the periodic table, and dates of historical events. Do you suppose those roots go deeply into the long-term memory banks of most students? What is the real result of all this effort?

Use yourself as a test case:

- Can you name all the presidents?
- Can you name all the state capitals?
- Do you know the all the elements on the periodic table?
- Can you remember when the Missouri Compromise was signed?

How'd you do? Did some of that information fall on rocky ground in your earlier years? "Since they have no root, they last only a short time."

There has to be a better way to conduct the learning process. Neither the schools nor the church can afford to cast so many seeds wastefully on such rocky ground.

"I never let schooling interfere
with my education."

MARK TWAIN

How the Brain Works

If we want to understand learning and retention, we need some basic understanding of the human brain. This mass of gray matter is surely among the most wondrous of God's incredible creations. Its design, function, capabilities, and complexity are beyond compare to anything on earth. Only recently have biologists and neuroscientists begun to comprehend some of the workings of this miraculous processor of information, ideas, feelings, and faith.

How the brain retains information is itself a complex procedure.

Neural networks at several different brain locations may handle a single act of memory. The content of a learning event (what happened) is processed in a separate place from the event's meaning (how it felt). The names of things may be stored in various locations. Words, sounds, and records of visual pictures are all stored in different spots. No wonder our minds get a little jumbled sometimes!

The brain is different from a computer. But thinking about some of the operations of a computer can help us understand the workings of the brain. Like a typical computer, the brain possesses two basic types of memory—working memory and long-term memory. Similarly, a computer is equipped with RAM or random access memory for temporary tasking, and a hard drive for storing long-term data.

Scientists are finding that the human brain does not permanently store everything it encounters. Most of the information we receive lingers only temporarily in short-term memory, and then it simply evaporates. Data such as someone's phone number may reside long enough for us to dial the number, but then disappears, never making the transition into long-term memory. Just like a computer's RAM memory, we're able to temporarily work with information that is not permanently stored.

Information that makes it to the brain's long-term memory is lodged in a complex network of 10 billion nerve cells in the outer layer of the brain, called the cortex (our hard drive!). But even here information that does not get used can fade away. "Use it or lose it" is a meaningful phrase in brain science.

What determines whether something gets stored long-term? There's a small part in the center of the brain called the hippocampus. It acts as a gatekeeper, sorting information that will be held only a short time from the other information that will make the successful leap to long-term memory.

Ronald Kotulak, author of *Inside the Brain,* writes: "The

hippocampus is the Grand Central Station of memory. It dispatches arriving trains of thoughts to either short commuter runs that are quickly forgotten—phone numbers, names of party guests—or to more permanent destinations in the brain where important things like your home address, spouse's name, and the Second Law of Thermodynamics are stored."[1]

But how does the hippocampus decide? New research is shedding some light. If we can understand some of these secrets, we'll be more effective at helping people learn Bible truths long-term.

How do memories become permanent? Colin Rose and Malcolm Nicholl, authors of *Accelerated Learning for the 21st Century,* write: "It's largely dependent on how strongly the information is registered in the first place. That's why it's so important to learn in ways that involve hearing, seeing, saying, and doing and which involve positive emotions such as when we learn collaboratively. All factors that create strong memories."[2]

Scientists now believe that emotions are one of the primary factors that push information into long-term memory. We'll dig more deeply into the learning impact of emotions in the next chapter.

The Power of Association

The brain's hippocampus strives to make associations. When it encounters new information, it immediately asks, "How is this like something I already know?" When it successfully finds a related link, it begins to capture and store the new information. Picture the mind as a library of books. A library's similar books are shelved together to help readers find the desired volumes. Imagine the difficulty if books in a library were stored haphazardly or illogically. Grouping books together by subject and author makes retrieval quick and easy. The human brain works similarly.

"The mind's cross-indexing
puts the best librarian to shame."

SHARON BEGLEY

Our travels take us to many parts of the world, including some very out-of-the-way spots. A few years ago we visited Indonesian Irian Jaya, which occupies the western half of New Guinea. There we trekked with our son, Matt, into the highlands to visit the primitive Dani people who are just now emerging from the Stone Age. The women wear only crude woven skirts. The men wear only dried gourds to cover their private parts.

We were awed by these people and their lifestyle. We struggled to understand what life is like for them. Matt wondered if the men ever got embarrassed wearing only a gourd. Our expedition guide and interpreter, Koos, explained, "Oh, I've seen them get very embarrassed. But it's when they lose their gourds. They feel naked!" It was then that Matt (and his parents) made a connection, an association, with the Dani gourds. We knew the embarrassment of being caught without clothes. The new information about the Dani people—linked to other information we already knew—helped us to understand these people and their attire.

We've never forgotten those gourds. They're stored in our long-term memory banks, right next to the file on pants.

Jesus used the power of association constantly in his teaching. He knew the workings of the brain. Look at some examples:

- "You are the salt of the earth" (Matthew 5:13a).
- "You are the light of the world" (Matthew 5:14a).
- "For where your treasure is, there your heart will be also" (Matthew 6:21).

- "The eye is the lamp of the body" (Matthew 6:22a).
- "No one can serve two masters" (Matthew 6:24a).
- "A tree is recognized by its fruit" (Matthew 12:33b).
- "All who draw the sword will die by the sword" (Matthew 26:52b).

Jesus knew people would understand and retain the learning longer if he began his lessons with what they already knew. He linked the commonly known to his new concepts. To do so he often used objects as visual aids—things such as fish, boats, nets, sheep, and coins—to help his people understand and remember.

You can do the same today. With learners of any age, you can encourage more long-term learning by using objects that learners can associate with other parts of their lives. For instance, you could use a rubber band to launch a discussion on "stretching the truth." Ask learners to hold a rubber band with a partner. Instruct them to alternate telling "little white lies," stretching the rubber band tighter between them each time they lie. They'll experience what happens when a rubber band is stretched too far. This exercise builds on what people already know about rubber bands. Your follow-up discussion questions will link knowledge about rubber bands to new insights about the destructiveness of lying.

The debriefing questions we place after our active-learning experiences always include an interpretation question to link what students already know to the new learning of the day. For example, after the rubber band activity we might ask, "How is this rubber-band-stretching experience like or unlike telling a series of lies?" That's using the power of association to help people learn and retain.

Objects serve not only as associative links of information, but as ongoing reminders of new learning. Whenever learners use a rubber band in the future, their memories may link with the "stretching the truth" exercise. Your "thou shalt not lie" lesson then gets automatically reviewed time after time.

Learning through association works. We produced a video titled *Making the Bible Easy to Teach* that includes an interview with a young girl named Abigail. She attends a Sunday school that uses Hands-On Bible Curriculum, which utilizes associative thinking through the active use of objects and play activities. We asked her if she could remember the lesson from the previous week. She quickly told us the lesson's biblical point. We asked her about lessons going back several weeks. She also knew them. Finally, when we asked about a lesson earlier in the previous month, she struggled. Then we asked, "Do you remember the gizmo you used?" That was all it took. Her memory kicked in and she associated that gizmo with the biblical point.[3]

The brain moves information into long-term memory when we start with what people already know.

METAPHORS AND THEMES

The building of long-term memories through association can flow throughout an entire learning experience. This is accomplished through focusing on a particular metaphor or theme and developing it. Think of vacation Bible school. This learning experience typically revolves around a central theme or setting, such as a cruise, a treasure hunt, or a safari. In the vacation Bible school curricula we design, we tie the theme into everything, including the recreation, all the music, every craft, all the video clips, each prayer, and even every snack. This connectivity is not only fun and attractive, it helps cement the learning.

Thematic settings work for learners of all ages. Look how theme parks use this approach to create memorable experiences for everyone. Hundreds of details—architecture, signs, textures, sounds, music, smells, and tastes all tie in to the theme. People connect. And they remember.

You can use this approach regularly to help people learn. For example, use a court case motif to lead learners through a session on Christian apologetics. Decorate the room to look like a courtroom. Cast a student as the judge. Dress him or her in a robe. Use a gavel. Appoint a jury. Introduce evidence. Let the jury decide the verdict.

The people at Educational Discoveries, national corporate trainers, use metaphors and themes in their workshops. They transform corporate training rooms into little baseball parks and lemonade stands to teach subjects such as accounting to business people. And their students love it! They say the themes offer three simultaneous and powerful tools:[4]

1. The ability to establish and maintain a learning context.
2. The ability to simplify and dramatize learning concepts.
3. The ability to create emotional connection with the content to deepen learning.

How can you use metaphors and themes with your next lessons, workshops, retreats, and sermons? Have some fun amplifying your messages by thematically linking your words, images, and environment. You'll see learning take root.

TELL A STORY

A metaphor helps learners understand one kind of thing in terms of another. Jesus taught extensively with metaphors. And he often took metaphors a step further and built them into stories known as parables.

The Parable of the Sower is a classic example. Here Jesus linked what people already knew—farming—with a new lesson about learning and applying God's Word. Jesus proved himself to be a great—and memorable—storyteller.

Who are the great storytellers of today? Some of the most skilled are movie-makers. The good ones know how to grab our attention, pull us along, deliver information, and move that information into long-term memory. How do they do that? René Schlaepfer, a pastor in California, outlined some of the filmmakers' storytelling secrets in Vital Ministry Magazine.[5] You can use these secrets to help people learn...

> **SIMPLICITY.** Don't complicate. Be able to describe your story in one line. With *Jaws* it was "Huge shark eats people." With *Titanic:* "Big ship sinks."
>
> **SUSPENSE.** It's the wondering-what's-going-to-happen-in-the-end that pulls people through a story.
>
> **SHARED EMOTION.** When you tap people's emotions, you lock them into the story.
>
> **SEAMLESS STORY.** Each story element flows into the next. This often requires cutting superfluous material.
>
> **SURPRISING START AND SUDDEN STOP.** Great movies bring you into the action before you know what's going on. And they end with a quick punch.

Now relate those storytelling secrets to one of Jesus' stories, the Prodigal Son (Luke 15:11-32), for example. Here's a story that's simple, suspenseful, emotion-packed, and seamless, with a surprising start and a sudden stop. Jesus knew the secrets to moving a story into people's long-term memories.

The next time you need to teach, don't simply dispense information. Tell a story. And don't be too tempted to always explain the story. Let your learners grapple with the story in their own ways. Allow the Holy Spirit to work within them. Jesus often told stories without explanations.

INTERVAL REINFORCEMENT

Bud the farmer knows what's needed for seeds to sprout and to continue growing until they bear fruit. "They need water—in the right amount—given to them over and over," he says. "You can't water a crop just once and expect it to survive." The secret: repeated doses of moisture, spread throughout the growing cycle. The same principle applies to learning.

If we want learning to stick, we need to "water" it; we need to reinforce the learning multiple times. At the opening of this chapter, one of the problems with the boy's learning was his lack of reinforcement. He studied a Bible verse once, got tested on it, and moved on to other things. Because he visited each verse only once and did not return to it, each one evaporated from his memory. It never made the leap from short-term memory to long-term memory.

Research shows that retention is dramatically increased by what's called "interval reinforcement"—review or use of the material repeatedly over a period of time. If the brain registers information just once, less than 10 percent of the message is likely to be remembered after 30 days. But if there are six exposures to the information over 30 days, 90 percent of the message is likely to be retained.[6] Think of it like watering a crop. Frequent, periodic rainfall or irrigation spread throughout the growing season produces a healthy crop.

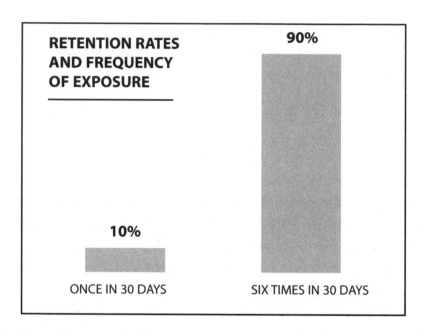

RETENTION RATES AND FREQUENCY OF EXPOSURE

90%

10%

ONCE IN 30 DAYS

SIX TIMES IN 30 DAYS

Dr. Barry Gordon, head of the memory-disorders clinic at Johns Hopkins School of Medicine, said, "What we think of as memories are ultimately patterns of connection among nerve cells." A cover story in Newsweek magazine explained further: "A newly encoded memory may involve thousands of neurons spanning the entire cortex. If it doesn't get used, it will quickly fade. But if we activate it repeatedly, the pattern of connection gets more and more deeply embedded in our tissue."[7]

Intuitively we know the principle of interval reinforcement to be true. If we hear a song just once, we're not likely to remember it. But if we hear it several times, it may reside in our memory forever. Similarly, if we meet someone just once, we may quickly forget the person's name. But if we interact with that person many times, we're likely to remember the person and his or her name.

So why is this simple principle so often ignored in the church? The problem lies, once again, in a misunderstanding of the difference between teaching and learning. Teachers and leaders have a strong desire to impart a lot of good information. The thought of returning to already-covered information seems a waste of time when there's so much new information to cover. "I need to teach much" overshadows "what are my students capable of absorbing?"

It's time we stop and ponder the sower. Bud knows he cannot increase his yield by spreading more seeds per square foot than anybody else. In fact, he'll tell you that too many seeds in one plot of ground will result in overcrowding, choking, and a miserable harvest. He plants only the number of seeds the plot can handle.

Pertaining to sharing God's message, Jesus knew this principle of the sower also. At one point in his ministry he said, "I have many more things to say to you, but they are too much for you now" (John 16:12, New Century Version). There's nothing to be gained by attempting to spray more information than people can handle.

Coverage is not the goal. Our time is much better spent covering less material, but covering it in a way that moves the material into long-term memory. In other words, teachers and leaders will be more effective not by attempting to plant more seeds, but by frequently watering the appropriate number of seeds. That's interval reinforcement.

You can utilize interval reinforcement by adopting a number of new habits. Here are some suggestions:

- Review main points frequently within each lesson or learning time.
- Address the point multiple times, using different approaches that appeal to different learning styles and intelligences.
- Reinforce the key point at the conclusion of the lesson.
- Review main points at the start of the next lesson.
- Once a month, review all key points from the previous thirty days.
- Allocate an entire session once a month to reinforce key points.

- Set aside a session every six months to review all key points from the previous six months.
- Take a few key concepts and emphasize them for a year, rather than tackling a new concept, verse, or story each week.
- Supply high quality materials for families to use during the week to review and reinforce the lesson points introduced at church. (More on this in Chapter 6.)

Group's FaithWeaver resources implement a careful series of interval reinforcements. The FaithWeaver Bible curriculum reinforces the main biblical point throughout each lesson, using key questions. All ages study the same Bible story in different age-appropriate ways. A special resource for home use allows families to reinforce the week's learning at home through devotions and fun activities. A children's church component weaves the same point through music and worship. Pastoral resources supply ideas for incorporating the lesson point into family worship time. And Faith-Weaver midweek resources weave and reinforce the point through fellowship and service activities. Learners of all ages internalize, remember, and apply the biblical points because they're imbedded in long-term memory through interval reinforcement.

"Children always take the line of most persistence."

MARCELENE COX

FIRST IMPRESSIONS, LAST IMPRESSIONS

Take a moment to try a little experiment from Rose and Nicholl's *Accelerated Learning for the 21st Century*.[8] Look at the list of words below. Relax and read through the words slowly—just once. When you reach the end, follow the next instructions.

Grass	Truth	Blue
Paper	Table	Sheep
Cat	Fork	Meaning
Knife	Zulu	Field
Love	Radio	Pencil
Bird	Wisdom	Stream
Tree	Flower	Pen

Now cover up the list and write down as many of the words as you can recall, in any order.

_____	_____	_____
_____	_____	_____
_____	_____	_____
_____	_____	_____
_____	_____	_____
_____	_____	_____
_____	_____	_____

Now, it doesn't matter how many you remembered. Compare your list to the original list. Do you notice anything in particular? Perhaps your list reflects the following:

YOU PROBABLY REMEMBERED THE FIRST WORDS. Does your list contain *grass* or *paper*? People tend to remember more of the beginning of any learning session.

YOU PROBABLY REMEMBERED THE LAST WORDS. Does your list contain *pen* or *stream*? People also tend to remember more of the end of a learning session.

What does this indicate to us? Recall is heightened at a learning session's start and end. First impressions are powerful. And last impressions are powerful. We can capitalize on this phenomenon by planning lots of beginnings and endings in our learning sessions. We can accomplish this by designing learning in shorter blocks and taking plenty of breaks.

Attention spans are short—in both children and adults. After only a few minutes, even with adults, minds wander. Adults are just more sophisticated in masking their wandering minds. We can enhance learning by planning short breaks and changes of direction every few minutes. Here are some suggestions to break up your learning segments:

- Stand and take three deep breaths.
- Toss out candy or other quick snacks.
- Reach for the ceiling and stretch.
- Serve ice water.
- Sing a simple, silly song.
- Toss a Kooshball around the room.
- Stand in a line and give back rubs.
- Play a quick game.
- Shake hands with a new friend.

● Switch teaching techniques—pair share, video clip, or active experience, for example.

The idea here is to take a refreshing rest from the brain intensity of learning. Your people will learn more and retain it longer when learning is conducted in shorter segments. Again, don't look upon such exercises as a waste of time. Time taken for well-paced breaks will increase learning. Remember, we're looking for maximum learning, not maximum teaching.

MUSIC AND MEMORY

Music, properly chosen and used, also increases learning and retention. Francis Rauscher at the University of California discovered that college students who listened to ten minutes of Mozart's Piano Sonata K 448 increased their spatial intelligence scores.

Rauscher also found that toddlers benefit from music. A group of preschool children who took music lessons performed far better on reasoning tests than other children who were not given music lessons.[9]

Appropriate background music can enhance learning. Bulgarian educational psychiatrist Dr. Georgi Lozanov found that listening to Baroque music, for instance, wields a mighty impact on our ability to absorb information and retain it.[10]

And we know that putting a message into song lyrics greatly improves retention. Even in the Middle Ages, monks employed music to help them memorize lengthy passages of Scripture.

Music helps us remember. If you doubt it, try to recall the content of the sermons you've heard over the past few years. Now try to recall the lyrics and tunes of songs, hymns, and choruses you've sung in church in recent years. Is your musical recall a bit more astute?

You can use the benefits of music frequently in your learning situations. Play appropriate background music when students are working on projects, during breaks, to set a mood, and while learners are arriving and departing. And use music to teach or emphasize a biblical point. Use it to make Scripture memory come naturally and enjoyably.

Had the boy at this chapter's beginning learned his Bible verses set to music, he no doubt could have recalled much, much more. God created us in wondrous ways. If we'll simply design our learning around his great design, we'll sow seeds that will grow.

"Music appeals to the heart,
whereas writing is addressed to the intellect;
it communicates directly, like perfume."

HONORE DE BALZAC

REFERENCES

1. Ronald Kotulak, *Inside the Brain* (Kansas City, MO: Andrews and McMeel, 1996), 135.

2. Colin Rose and Malcolm J. Nicholl, *Accelerated Learning for the 21st Century* (New York, NY: Delacorte Press, 1997), 48.

3. *Making the Bible Easy to Teach* (Loveland, CO: Group Publishing, 1998).

4. *The Designing Game* (Boulder, CO: Educational Discoveries, Inc., 1997), 51.

5. René Schlaepfer, "Secrets of the Cinema," Vital Ministry Magazine (July/August, 1998), 35.

6. Albert Mehrabian, *Silent Messages* (Belmont, CA: Wadsworth Publishing Company, 1980).

7. Geoffrey Cowley and Anne Underwood, "How Memory Works," Newsweek (June 15, 1998), 51.

8. Rose and Nicholl, *Accelerated Learning for the 21st Century*, 131-132.

9. Kotulak, *Inside the Brain*, 141.

10. Successful Learning Resources Guide for Educators, Parents and Families, "The Mozart Effect," Web site www.howtolearn.com/ndil2.html.

CHAPTER FIVE

Emotion: The Glue of Learning and Retention

Ralph Wright loves young children. For years he's taught the three-year-old Sunday school class at his church in Washington. He loves preschoolers' enthusiasm and imagination.

He takes full advantage of that imagination in his classes. He fully involves the children in Bible stories. They don't just hear about the story. They experience it firsthand!

One Sunday Ralph involved the kids in the story of Jesus calming the stormy waters. He prepared by outlining a boat's shape on the floor with masking tape. He placed blue fabric around the boat outline to suggest water.

One by one Ralph lifted the preschoolers into the pretend boat. Then he sat in a chair at the front of the boat and proceeded to teach the lesson in an active, adventurous way. He had the children rock back and forth pretending they were being tossed in a storm, just as the disciples were.

Then suddenly, unexpectedly, a little boy fell overboard! The rest of the kids shouted, "Help him! He can't swim!"

Ralph heroically jumped overboard and saved the child. Once they were safely back in the boat, the children talked about how they were frightened when the boy fell overboard. They realized how the disciples must have felt that night long ago. Ralph talked about how Jesus saves them. Then they all held hands and prayed, thanking Jesus for his protection over them. It was a powerful lesson.

But that's not the end of this story. Later in the week, the church got a call from a preschooler's parent who asked why Ralph hadn't obtained parental permission slips before taking the children on a boat ride! "We heard one of the boys even fell overboard," the parent said in all seriousness. The concerned mom was much relieved when she was told the children never left the classroom.

Whatever she heard from her child illustrates the power of lessons that evoke real feelings. Those kids experienced a boat ride and storm akin to the disciples' experience. They understood the lesson, and they'll likely remember it. "The kids got the lesson," said Ralph's wife, Sandi. "A coloring page would have never helped them learn the story like that boat ride experience!"

What made that lesson so powerful, so real, so unforgettable? The active ingredient here was emotion. Those children's emotions pulled them into the story, activated their imaginations, piqued their curiosity about how Jesus saves and protects, and cemented the lesson into their long-term memories.

But Ralph was not the first to implement emotions to teach that story. Jesus, the star of the story, helped his disciples in just the same way. Wasn't it the emotion of fear that grabbed the disciples' attention? Wasn't it the emotion of terror that drove them to wake Jesus and say, "Lord, save us! We're going to drown!"? Wasn't it the emotion of amazement that caused the disciples to ask, "What kind of man is this? Even the winds and waves obey him" (Matthew 8:25, 27)?

Those men learned a powerful lesson that night. The intensity of their emotions anchored that experience and its meaning in their long-term memories. The roots of their learning reached deeply into their minds and souls. These seeds did not fall on rocky ground.

*"Human beings are full of emotion,
and the teacher who knows how to use it
will have dedicated learners."*

LEON LESSINGER

OUR EMOTIONAL MIND

We mentioned in the last chapter that the brain's hippocampus regulates what gets stored in long- and short-term memory. The hippocampus tends to push information toward long-term memory if it can associate the data with something it already knows. But association is not its only filter. Scientists believe the other major filter is emotion.

We tend to remember more when our emotions are engaged. The brain is more prone to retain the sensational than the mundane. Think back to your last vacation. What do you remember from that time? Chances are your strongest memories are tied to strong emotions. Perhaps it was the emotion of awe at seeing a spectacular sight. Or the emotion of fear at testing a new adventurous activity. Or the emotion of love at reconnecting with family members. Or the emotion of frustration when the car broke down. Emotions drive what we remember.

In our travels, we've met many people from diverse cultures. But we've noticed that people all over the globe are basically the same. God created them all with a similar set of emotions. The basic emotions of joy, anger, fear, and sadness look amazingly the same everywhere. We've found the same emotion-driven reactions and looks on people's faces in the hill tribes of northern Thailand, in the native peoples of the Amazon basin, in Eskimo families above the Arctic Circle, in the Bedouin cultures in the Middle East, and in the primitive tribes in New Guinea.

We learned later that a University of California researcher, Paul Ekman, made discoveries of core emotions around the world. In fact, he conducted some of his research among remote tribes in New Guinea. These preliterate people were untainted by cinema or television. But they displayed the same facial expressions for happiness, fear, anger, and sadness as their counterparts anywhere else on earth. And, when shown photos of other people bearing these expressions, the New Guinea tribespeople identified the emotions with perfect precision.[1]

God created us all with feelings, emotions. And those emotions influence our behavior. Scientists know there are more neural connections going *from* the emotional part of the brain *to* the intellectual part than vice versa. That's why our emotions are often more powerful than logic in influencing our behavior. (Now you know how those church committees can make such illogical, emotional decisions!)

Two Minds in One

People often talk about "letting the heart lead" even when the logical analysis would lead elsewhere. Regardless what the cold, hard facts might indicate, people often opt to do "what feels right."

This is true not only with individuals, but with masses within society. Can you think of elections and ballot issues that have been ultimately decided not by logic but by emotion?

Other times emotions may gallop toward a certain decision, only to get stopped and cooled by rational thinking. Anger sometimes flares within us, causing us to rehearse over and over how we'll verbally assault an offending person. But then the rational mind overtakes the emotion and causes us to change our approach.

It's as if we have two minds. Daniel Goleman, author of the groundbreaking book *Emotional Intelligence,* writes:

> In a very real sense we have two minds, one that thinks and one that feels...These two minds, the emotional and the rational, operate in tight harmony for the most part, intertwining their very different ways of knowing to guide us through the world. Ordinarily there is a balance between emotional and rational minds, with emotion feeding into and informing the operations of the rational mind, and the rational mind refining and sometimes vetoing the inputs of the emotions...But when passions surge the balance tips: it is the emotional mind that captures the upper hand, swamping the rational mind.[2]

UNCOMFORTABLE FEELINGS ABOUT FEELINGS

For many years we've advocated acknowledging and applying emotions in the learning process. Our resources often include activities that evoke emotions. And our debriefing process typically includes questions about learners' reactions, about their feelings. But our critics sometimes say, "I don't like that feeling stuff. Bible study shouldn't be based on feelings."

We agree that Bible study shouldn't be based on feelings. But we believe feelings play a role, whether we like it or not, in everyone's learning process. So we're better off acknowledging and applying emotions rather than trying to pretend they don't exist.

*"We know emotion is very important
to the educative process because it drives attention,
which drives learning and memory...
It's impossible to separate emotion
from the important activities of life.
Don't even try."*

ROBERT SYLWESTER, PROFESSOR
UNIVERSITY OF OREGON

Emotion is the glue of learning and retention. Many years ago we escaped for what we hoped would be a relaxing weekend at Lake Tahoe. Our son, Matt, then two years old, stayed with Thom's parents in Colorado. At dawn that Sunday the hotel phone intruded upon our sleep. It was Thom's mother: "We're at the hospital with Matt. Something is terribly wrong. He's not moving."

Our minds splintered with anxiety and a sense of helplessness. We sat up in bed and immediately started to pray. "Oh, God, touch that little boy. Make him well!"

We quickly got dressed, raced out of the hotel, and caught the next plane to Colorado. Thankfully, by the time we arrived home, Matt was fine. The doctors said some head congestion apparently caused him to turn very lethargic. It was his way of coping with the common cold.

The emotional intensity of that time will never leave our memories. But it's not only the emotions we'll remember. Hundreds of details about that day are indelibly set in our minds as well. We can tell you exactly how that hotel room looked, where the phone was located, how the bathroom was arranged. We can tell you exactly what and how we prayed. We can quote what the airline representative said when we explained our need to change our reservation. We can describe for you how we swept up and clutched a bewildered two-year-old boy the moment we got home. We remember it all because of the powerful impact of the emotions.

Emotion is the glue of learning and retention. That's how God created us. We remember not only the emotion but the information surrounding it. Test yourself on this. Do you remember where you went on your first date? What was the date's name? What did the place look like? Do you remember where you were when you heard the news of the explosion of the space shuttle Challenger? Who was with you? How did people react?

Emotions of all sorts gather and send loads of information into our memory banks. Our memories are seared by fear, joy, anger, disgust, hilarity, surprise, sadness, love, frustration, worry, wonder, and dozens of other emotions.

Some of these emotions occur in Christian education settings, whether we want them to or not. It is not possible for us to prevent learners from experiencing emotions. They will. Even if a teacher stands and lectures, some learners will experience emotions, although their feelings may not enhance the desired learning.

We believe it's more effective to acknowledge that all learners experience emotions, and they connect with their emotions to help cement important biblical truths to their hearts. So we like to design learning activities that evoke particular emotional responses in learners. The paper-doll tearing activity we explained in Chapter 2 evokes feelings first of aggression then of tenderness as participants try to reassemble the torn doll. Then they debrief how they were feeling and associate those emotions with real-life situations. Many learners experience powerful reactions to this exercise. They remember it and the biblical discoveries attached to it. Years later people often approach us and recall this experience.

That happens to us all the time. Former students often stop us and say, "Remember about ten years ago when you led that activity..."

They remember long-term because they were touched deeply through their emotional minds.

In the same way, Ralph's little preschoolers will probably return to him years from now and say, "Remember when you put us in that make-believe boat and one kid fell overboard in the storm?" Similarly, we're certain Jesus' disciples recalled among themselves years later about the frightening night when their Lord calmed the water.

"You cannot know what you do not feel."

MARYA MANNES

JESUS AND EMOTIONS

Can we legitimately apply human emotions in the learning process—to help people grow in their faith? What clues can we observe in the ministry of Jesus?

Jesus knew the minds of his followers. He knew how those minds worked, how they were affected and chiseled by emotions. He let those emotions work toward his purpose.

On the lake that stormy night, the disciples' emotion of fear helped cement a lesson of faith (Matthew 8:23-27).

Later, Jesus again created a memorable experience through the disciples' fear and amazement when he walked on water. And Peter learned about the tension between fear and faith when he attempted to walk on the water himself (Matthew 14:25-32).

Examples of emotion-laden learning experiences abound throughout Jesus' ministry:

- The angst of the villagers who learned of Jesus' role in the suicidal pig plunge (Matthew 8:28-34).
- The consternation of the Pharisees when the disciples picked grain on the Sabbath (Matthew 12:1-8).
- The sadness of the rich young man (Matthew 19:16-22).
- The indignation of the disciples when the woman anointed Jesus with expensive perfume (Matthew 26:6-13).
- The frenzy of Martha (Luke 10:38-42).
- The discomfort of the disciples when Jesus washed their feet (John 13:1-17).

Emotions soaked all of these episodes and many more. The intense emotions guaranteed that no one forgot these experiences or the spiritual messages attached to them.

We have no evidence that Jesus tried to avoid the occurrence of emotions in his teaching and learning opportunities. In fact, he often seemed to knowingly provoke strong feelings. He knew the power of those feelings for learning.

If Jesus could make fruitful use of human emotions, so might we.

EMOTIONS THAT DON'T ENHANCE GOOD LEARNING

Not all emotional responses help students learn the lesson of the day. Some emotions can be counterproductive in a classroom setting. If learners arrive with unresolved emotions such as anger, anxiety, or depression, they're not likely to absorb your lesson information.

Daniel Goleman writes:

Powerful negative emotions twist attention toward their own preoccupations, interfering with the attempt to focus elsewhere. Indeed, one of the signs that feelings have veered over the line into the pathological is that they are so intrusive they overwhelm all other thought, continually sabotaging attempts to pay attention to whatever other task is at hand. For the person going through an upsetting divorce—or the child whose parents are—the mind does not stay long on the comparatively trivial routines of the work or school day.[3]

We can learn from this that we must approach students' emotional minds carefully. Just as some emotions help cement spiritual truths, other emotions can block positive learning. And we need to learn to be highly sensitive to each learner's emotional state of mind. The more attuned we are the more effective our teaching will be. Learners' emotions are real, even if we think they're sometimes inappropriate. Those feelings exist, and they're often very powerful, for better or worse.

Because of the significant role emotions play in every person, we must avoid inappropriately manipulating them. In this chapter's opening story, Ralph invited his preschoolers to experience the disciples' fear in a make-believe way. That was appropriate. It would have been inappropriate to provoke fear by threatening the children with a weapon. That approach would certainly have resulted in memorable feelings of fear, but it would have crossed the line into unhealthy manipulation.

DISCIPLINE AND EMOTIONS

In our work with children's ministry people, the most requested training topic is usually classroom discipline. We often wonder exactly what teachers have in mind when they make these requests. Ultimately, what are they most seeking—control of the classroom or maximum student learning?

Since we contend that emotions are closely linked to learning, we must inquire about student emotions connected to disciplinary actions. This is important because in many church settings the most intense—and thus the most memorable—emotions arise from teacher-driven disciplinary action.

Little Jimmy will quickly forget all those word-puzzle worksheets and those coloring pages and the flannelgraph lectures—because they stir very little emotion and they're largely irrelevant to his life. But when he gets bored with these tedious exercises and begins to bother other kids and the teacher, watch closely. If the teacher erupts in anger and embarrasses Jimmy in front of the other children, Jimmy's emotions now turn red-hot. This scene is now being permanently stored in his long-term memory. Church, Sunday school—and perhaps God and the Bible—get registered as unpleasant, unfair, and punitive.

Unfortunately, many teachers' most prolific classroom application of emotion comes in the context of discipline. It is here they display their own most intense emotions. And it is here their students feel the greatest emotional impact. The result of most of this emotional energy is usually not positive. It's not positive for the noncompliant child, nor for the rest of the class, nor for the teacher.

Consider the not-so-hidden messages in some of the disciplinary techniques employed by some church teachers. Jimmy continues to talk after the teacher tells him to stop. So the teacher, with desperation in her voice, says, "OK, Jimmy, that's it. If you can't be quiet and work on your worksheet, then you have to sit with the girls!" You may be assured that Jimmy's sponge-like emotional mind is now in full intake mode. What's he learning here? What's he learning about church? What's he learning about girls? And what are the girls learning from this teacher's message? For everyone in the room, this emotional moment will be the most remembered event from the class.

Teachers devise all sorts of disciplinary techniques. Another emotion-packed tactic is the use of public sin scorekeeping. Amy repeatedly pokes the child in front of her. Every time she does it, the teacher makes another mark beside her name on the chalkboard. Soon Amy's sin score reaches an all-time class record. The other kids hiss and boo. Amy doesn't know whether to shrink or take some ironic pride in setting a record. What will Amy remember about this class? What will the others remember? Will the bland worksheets stand a chance of being remembered longer than Amy's public sin listing?

Then there's the timeout chair—the contemporary equivalent of the dunce's throne. Michael seems to get sentenced to this dubious spot every week. He'd rather be anywhere but Sunday school, but his parents make him attend. He's learning a lot—about humiliation. As soon as he's old enough to make his own decisions, he's already determined he'll never come to church again.

Alternatives to Punishing Emotions

Simply put, disciplinary punishments often evoke negative feelings that fester in students' long-term memories. Jody Capehart, Gordon West, and Becki West discuss better alternatives in their book *The Discipline Guide for Children's Ministry.* They write:

> The bottom line is this: How children feel about class affects how and what they learn. In fact, a child's feelings about a Sunday school class will last much longer than the memory of

Bible-story facts. In the Sunday school class, we need to be aware of how kids are feeling. As you're teaching, monitor your students' responses. After class, ask yourself these questions:

● Was this class a pleasant or unpleasant experience for the children?

● Were they excited about what they were learning?

● Did I treat each child with respect, kindness, and concern?

● Could they make the connection between the lesson and real life?

● Did I (or another adult or student) refrain from saying anything that might have been taken as criticism, humiliation, or a put-down?[4]

We're afraid many teachers who seek advice on handling disciplinary problems are looking in the wrong direction. They tend to blame the students, or the parents, or the media, or society in general. But in Christian education settings, those things are seldom the leading cause of inappropriate behavior. The main culprit is often the curriculum. If the curriculum fails to captivate the students, their active minds will look elsewhere for stimulation. And that often leads to disruptive behavior.

"Let's be honest," says Alfie Kohn, author of *Beyond Discipline*. "Students frequently perceive the tasks they are given as not worth doing—and sometimes with good reason. Worksheets and textbooks and lectures are often hard to justify pedagogically...One of my own major (albeit belated) revelations as a teacher was that behavior problems in my classroom were not due to students' unnatural need for attention or power. The students were acting up mostly to make the time pass faster...Back then, I was thinking about a new approach to discipline. What I really needed was a new curriculum."[5]

Recognizing that most behavior problems in children's classes are caused by student boredom, we've devoted our lives to creating curriculum that engages and captivates students. And the results have been gratifying. We sent a camera crew to visit churches around the country using our Hands-On Bible Curriculum. One of the questions our interviewer asked teachers was, "How do you handle discipline problems in your class?" Every teacher replied basically the same way: "We really don't have discipline problems. The kids are so engaged they don't have time or desire to act up."

Alfie Kohn sums it up well: "When students are 'off task,' our first response should be to ask, 'What's the task?' "[6]

Making Learning Emotive

We know that emotions are major drivers of what students learn, retain, and apply in their lives. We've learned that some emotions can be counterproductive; they inhibit positive learning. Other emotions in an educational setting can send the good news into long-term memory where it can be referenced for a lifetime.

You can insert opportunities for your students of any age to experience emotions that will enhance their learning. Instead of telling students about a Bible story, try letting them experience it. In so doing, you'll recapture some of the emotional punch felt by the original characters in Bible times.

We've designed Bible re-creations using a huge plastic bubble into which students crawl. We start with big sheets of thin black plastic that are often used as ground cover by landscapers. Using duct tape, we tape the edges to the floor, leaving slack in the middle of the plastic sheeting. At one end of this envelope we insert an electric box fan. It inflates the envelope, creating a big puffy bubble. At the opposite end, we cut a slit through which the students enter.

We've conducted all sorts of learning sessions inside these big bubbles. For children in vacation Bible school, the space became the inside of Jonah's giant fish. At another time, it became the dark hold of the apostle Paul's prisoner ship. Those children experienced the Bible stories! Their emotions kicked into high gear, searing their learning into long-term memory.

We've also used the big bubble with teenagers and adults. At our workcamps we transformed the bubble into the tomb where Jesus' body was placed. Workcampers were invited in to pray and to witness that the body was gone. "He is risen," we whispered. Many campers were moved to tears as they knelt inside the dark tomb and contemplated the sacrifice of their Lord. The lesson became real, permanently nailed to their souls through the intense emotion of experiencing the story.

Our new FaithWeaver Bible Curriculum uses this technique of placing students inside the Bible stories. All students become actively involved. Think of it as an expedition. Students don't merely read about the expedition, or fill in a worksheet about it, or listen to someone else talk about it. They actually join the expedition. They become part of the story. They crawl inside the Scripture. They feel it. And those feelings ensure they'll remember it—for good.

Using Empathy Factors

Emotions can be constructively evoked through learning games and simulations. These classroom experiences engage students in intriguing situations that pique emotions that can later be discussed.

With adults and teenagers we use a learning game involving a candle. We ask the group to divide in half and stand in two lines facing one another. We then hand the lighted candle to one student and instruct him or her to walk or run through the gauntlet formed by the others. We instruct the group to try to blow out the candle. The object is for the candle-carrier to make it all the way through with the candle still lit. Everyone gets a chance to carry the candle.

It's a difficult exercise. The learners often feel frustration or determination as they try different methods to keep their candles lit.

During our debriefing time we direct the learners' attention to Matthew 5:14-15:

> "You are the light of the world. A city on a hill cannot be hidden. Neither do people light a lamp and put it under a bowl. Instead they put it on its stand, and it gives light to everyone in the house."

We ask how this game is like or unlike being a light for God. Emotions again emerge as students relate how their peers sometimes try to snuff out their spiritual lights. But they remember that even in the game, someone always stood by to relight their candles. That's just like God! He's always there to reignite our faith and strengthen us to go back out into the world to spread his light.

Such symbolic learning situations evoke emotions that ensure learning. Jesus used this technique when he washed the disciples' feet. Those men experienced a powerful symbolic lesson of humble servanthood. Their heightened emotions intensified their learning and retention.

How does a teacher go about designing learning simulations and games that evoke teachable emotions? We begin by analyzing what biblical point we wish to explore. We identify a particular emotion—or "empathy factor"—that may help solidify the learning.

Let's say we wish to increase students' care for the poor. We may choose to create feelings of neediness, or perhaps of compassion, or the joy of servanthood. Then we design an experience that evokes one or more of those empathy factors.

We might serve yummy refreshments to just half the class. That would create feelings of neediness among the have-nots and perhaps feelings of superiority among the well-fed. After the simulation, we'd conduct a debriefing time to allow students to get in touch with their emotions and associate them with real-life situations.

Emotional involvement causes the roots of learning to penetrate deeply into long-term memory. God created us as emotional beings. Jesus' teaching evoked strong emotions. Those strong emotions helped make his lessons unforgettable. We too can teach as Jesus taught.

"The greatest insights happen to us in moments of awe."

ABRAHAM JOSHUA HESCHEL

REFERENCES

1. Daniel Goleman, *Emotional Intelligence* (New York, NY: Bantam, 1995), 290.

2. Goleman, *Emotional Intelligence,* 8-9.

3. Goleman, *Emotional Intelligence,* 78-79.

4. Jody Capehart, Gordon West, and Becki West, *The Discipline Guide for Children's Ministry* (Loveland, CO: Group Publishing, 1997), 21.

5. Alfie Kohn, *Beyond Discipline* (Alexandria, VA: Association for Supervision and Curriculum Development, 1996), 19.

6. Kohn, *Beyond Discipline,* 19.

CHAPTER SIX

FAMILIES: WHERE ROOTS GO DEEP

Growing up on a farm, Joani learned early the meaning of faith. Each year her dad, Bud, would begin the process: preparing the soil, planting the seeds, cultivating the crops, and harvesting the grain. But life on the farm wasn't always that smooth. Every week the family would watch the sky and give thanks for receiving just the right amount of rain and sunshine to grow the crops. Other times they'd struggle, for nature didn't always deliver prosperity. Sometimes ominous tornado clouds loomed. Other times hail shredded fledgling greenery. And occasionally life-giving rain overdosed into torrents of devastating flood water.

Growing up on the farm involved more than agriculture. Joani saw how her parents dealt with success and failure. She learned how faith in God put life in perspective. By watching her dad work unceasingly from dawn to dark—but always making Sunday a day of rest—she learned the importance of worship and remembering the Sabbath day to keep it holy. She watched her mom live with a heart of love and compassion, serving wherever anyone was needed. Visits to the nursing home with her mom taught that caring for the needy was a way of life. Whenever a neighbor had a special need, Joani's parents were there (and still are today!). Her family was fertile soil where the roots of faith grew deep.

With all our writing about Christian education and learning in the church, we simply can't ignore the family's impact on faith formation. As much as we can do in a church classroom, we have to admit there's an even more powerful learning setting: the family. Most church workers would agree that parents wield the greatest impact on their child's morals, values, and faith. And that power can go either way. Parents can either impact their children's faith growth positively, or sadly, just as powerfully, negatively.

So what does this mean for the church?

CHURCH AND FAMILIES

In the old days, families survived because of self-sufficiency. Then families began relinquishing responsibilities. One turning point could have been when society decided that compulsory public education would better suit the nation. So teaching that formerly happened in the home moved to the public classroom. Gradually our society became attracted to outsourcing and specialization!

As time went on though, we in the church mirrored the idea of specialization. Most parents have gladly handed over their children's Christian education to the church—and the church has nobly tried to shoulder the responsibility. Most moms and dads feel woefully inadequate when it comes to nuances of theology and doctrine. Some have even waved goodbye to teaching Christian values in the home. Could it be that everything has become so specialized and compartmentalized that we've done the same to our faith? Has Christianity in families fallen prey to compartmentalization along with Starbucks coffee and manicure salons?

Faith at its essence is a relationship. And although we can experience and learn more about that relationship at church—our lives, particularly our family lives, are the laboratory for living out our beliefs.

Often we both marvel at how our families shaped who we are and how we understand our relationship with God. Here's just one example: We both enjoy working together as a team—not only as husband and wife, but also as co-workers at Group Publishing—even writing books together!

Lots of people ask us how we can work together. Some are even baffled by how much we actually enjoy it! Yet we both realize we were trained by our parents. We both learned from our families how to do that. Both sets of parents taught us how to be married—and work together as a team. Joani's parents labored as farmers and Thom's parents built a retail music business. Even though we didn't know it at the time, we were watching and learning as our moms and dads communicated, worked out differences, made decisions, and supported and respected each other. We saw Ephesians 5:31-33 in action:

" 'For this reason a man will leave his father and mother and be united to his wife, and the two will become one flesh.' This is a profound mystery—but I am talking about Christ and the church. However, each one of you also must love his wife as he loves himself, and the wife must respect her husband."

Our parents taught us mutual respect for each other as husband and wife. We witnessed the way Paul described Jesus' relationship with the church. Now our parents didn't overtly point out those verses, but they were teaching them! That's the power of families' influence on how one views what a relationship with God must be like.

We know living in a household centered on Christ may be a rare blessing these days. But we can't underestimate the powerful education that happens at home as invaluable and life-shaping. Just hearing the Gospel message an hour on Sunday or in Sunday school class pales in comparison to a family living out their Christian faith twenty-four hours a day.

Think about your own family. What did you learn about Jesus through your parent(s)? Was God a loving and forgiving father? Or was God a policeman in the sky, ready to squish you when you made a mistake? Was the church a foreign entity—or was it a comfortable haven of support? Was stewardship a way of life—giving to others what God has first given to you—or was the complaint around the Sunday dinner, "Why are they always begging for money at church?" (That is, if your family even attended church!)

Families are fertile soil for growing values and beliefs. As we talk with hundreds of ministers across the country, they all long for ways of effectively reaching families. We in the church must admit that's where faith will thrive—or be stunted.

So parents indeed are God's design for passing along the faith for generations. It's sobering: "For I, the Lord your God, am a jealous God, punishing the children for the sin of the fathers to the third and fourth generation of those who hate me, but showing love to a thousand generations of those who love me and keep my commandments" (Exodus 20:5b-6).

In *The Family-Friendly Church,* Ben Freudenburg and Rick Lawrence write: "Parents are the primary Christian educators in the church, and the family is the God-ordained institution for building faith in young people and for passing faith on from one generation to the next." [1]

Scripture tells us of the long-term, generation-to-generation impact of families. From an educational perspective, why is this so?

FAMILY MEMORIES TAKE DEEP ROOTS

Intense family memories lock in learning. That's because memories stick when emotion is attached. (Remember Chapter 5?)

For example, take a moment to ponder your own family life (as a child or now). What did you learn about these qualities?

love	goodness	patience
joy	faithfulness	kindness
peace	gentleness	self-control

Or what did you learn in your family about these things?

sexual immorality	fits of rage
impurity	selfish ambition
debauchery	dissensions
idolatry	factions
witchcraft	envy
hatred	drunkenness
discord	orgies
jealousy	

Do specific examples from these words from Galatians 5:19-23 pop into your mind? For many of these words, a vivid memory emerges because strong emotions are attached.

Even when people haven't lived in a Christian environment, they still "learned" something about life and values. It may or may not be what those of us in the church would hope is taught, but it was learned nonetheless.

Search Institute produced a landmark study called *Effective Christian Education: A National Study of Protestant Congregations.* Within the study lies a profound message for church educators. Search discovered what factors were involved in producing people who now profess a mature faith. Here's what they found:

● TALK WITH MOTHER. Analysis of the results of this study reveal that certain personal experiences have a measurable positive impact on the maturity of faith of the believer. The most powerful of these experiences is conversation about God with one's mother during the ages of 5 through 12. But among the five mainline denominations' 16- to 18-year-olds, almost 40 percent say that that event rarely or never occurred for them. Among adults, 26 percent did not have that experience in childhood.

● **TALK WITH FATHER, RELATIVES, FRIENDS.** Talking with one's father about faith or about God at the ages of 13 to 15 is another powerful correlate with maturity of faith, but 56 percent say this has occurred rarely or never for them. Other powerful experiences as a child or youth are such things as talking with other relatives about faith, the experience of having family devotions, engaging in family projects to help others, and, at the current moment, the number of friends who have strong religious interests.[2]

If this is true, what are we doing to help? How can we get families talking about their faith? Can we prompt conversations to take place between moms, dads, and kids?

We remember an example of how absolutely simple this can be: At the close of a youth group meeting, we handed out a photocopied list of open-ended questions to talk about at home. Nothing fancy. Nothing huge. Yet Chinh returned the following week describing the conversation she had with her mom. She reported that they shared in a way they'd never experienced before! As simply as providing families with "talk starter" questions, we can begin the process of seed planting that can go deep, that can last forever.

A key element of FaithWeaver curriculum offers a well-plotted approach to all ages studying the same Bible story each week. Then a resource page called "Driving Home the Point" reiterates the Bible story and gives easy, yet thought-provoking questions the whole family can talk about. Plus, the pastor can receive a resource that uses creative object lessons to tie the Bible stories to the sermon. Historically, the church has done a pretty good job of separating everyone so it's difficult for families to find a common conversation point! The churches that tie into FaithWeaver will reap the benefits of capitalizing on the family.

Another more recent study by Search Institute revealed forty developmental assets—both internal and external influences that can predict a young person's chance of having a happy, healthy life.[3] The study found that the more assets someone has, the less likely he or she will exhibit at-risk behavior. On the other hand, if a person doesn't have many of these assets, the more he or she will exhibit at-risk behavior.

As you read this list of positive resources that lead to healthy living, note how many involve family influence. Go ahead; place a check mark by those you think the family can influence.

1. Family support
2. Positive family communication
3. Other adult relationships
4. Caring neighborhood
5. Caring school climate
6. Parent involvement in schooling
7. A community that values youth
8. Youth used as resources
9. Service to others
10. Safety
11. Family boundaries
12. School boundaries
13. Neighborhood boundaries
14. Adult role models
15. Positive peer influence
16. High expectations
17. Creative activities
18. Youth programs
19. Religious community
20. Time at home
21. Achievement motivation
22. School engagement
23. Homework
24. Bonding to school
25. Reading for pleasure
26. Caring
27. Equality and social justice
28. Integrity
29. Honesty
30. Responsibility
31. Restraint
32. Planning and decision-making
33. Interpersonal competence

34. Cultural competence
35. Resistance skills
36. Peaceful conflict resolution
37. Personal power
38. Self-esteem
39. Sense of purpose
40. Positive view of personal future

UNDERSTANDING THE CHURCH'S ROLE

One could think all this "family impact" information diminishes the church's role in Christian education. To the contrary! The church, more than ever, is called to equip families to become havens where Christ's love shines. It just means that we in the church need to behave differently to capitalize on these hands-on faith laboratories. And life won't always look neat and tidy.

David M. Thomas, professor of family life studies at Regis University, writes in the Journal of Family Ministry:

> Knowing that the formation and education of persons was happening twenty-four hours a day, and they [religious educators] were with the children a mere one hour per week, what implications were there for sound and wise planning? Clearly this created an awareness which really complicated the life of the church. Families are messy and tend to mess up the careful planning of those who work with them. The disciples of Jesus saw some of their planned efficiency disappear when the Master called for the children to sit right next to him. Families are wonderful disturbers of comfortable and organized church events. [4]

It's this kind of thinking that is changing the church. Many age-specific ministers are transforming their jobs into some form of family ministry. Weary and frustrated by their short-term impact on kids, they're realizing it's time to partner with parents in the learning process. Plus, it means looking carefully at how they relate to parents and their role. Cutting-edge family ministers are passionate about redirecting the church's energies to families.

Ben Freudenburg says, "That's why I'm convinced we must shift from a church-centered, home-supported ministry model to a home-centered, church-supported ministry model."[5] (If you want to rethink your church's role with families, use *The Family-Friendly Church* as a powerful tool in sorting out how to get started and where to head!)

Not only is the church recognizing the need to influence families more deeply, the culture is searching to fill a spiritual void. Paging through the paper one Sunday, we were struck by an article in USA Weekend. The headline blared, "Dream Home 2000." Oh, that sounded good! So we read on. It described today's three top trends in home design that the author termed "future-proofing."[6]

The first wasn't that surprising:

HIDDEN HIGH-TECH for homes super-wired for 21st Century inventions: a central computer that controls everything, from lights to lawn sprinklers; super-fast cables for connecting remotely to your office or quickly to digital entertainment.

The second reflected more of a family feel:

HOUSES THAT GROW WITH US and change with our needs. Builders call this home trend "aging in place," and they're meeting it with features that accommodate Junior, Grandma and everyone in between.

The third trend took us off guard. What does this trend mean for the church, for family ministry?

ROOM FOR REFLECTION to fulfill the growing desire for the spiritual in everyday life. Thus, the trend toward home altars—spiritual centers architectural historian Jean McMann says honor "Something greater than ourselves."

We wondered: Is the church as tuned in as this architectural historian to the spiritual desires of today's families? Like the colored glass pieces at the end of a kaleidoscope, if we'd just twist and turn them a bit, we'd create a dazzling new image of the church and its families. We could help create homes where roots of faith can grow deep. What does that look like?

WAYS TO HELP THE ROOTS GO DEEPER

Reaching families and supporting them in Christian educational efforts doesn't have to be overwhelming—it just involves a new way of thinking. We believe you'll find parents welcoming the church's overtures to create family time together. George Barna, president of Barna Research Group, Ltd., reported in a news release that "One of the greatest needs expressed by adults is to have a healthy, happy and successful family. Millions of adults, however, do not believe that they are as successful in this effort as they wish to be. And despite the fact that four out of five Protestant churches (80%) offer specific family-oriented ministry, most adults indicate that those programs and ministry efforts achieve only a marginal positive impact among their families."

But here's the good news: "Nearly two-third of parents (63%) said that their church should take on an increased role in assisting parents...Among parents who are born again Christians, the opportunity is even greater: more than 8 out of 10 (81%) claimed that their church should be more involved in helping them be better parents." Interestingly, parents weren't as keen about looking to public schools or government for help. [7]

Parents do want help from the church. These ideas help parents see homes as fertile soil for God's Word to grow:

1. Help families reclaim mealtime. Maybe that means providing a time for families to eat together at church. Or maybe that means encouraging families to set aside certain meals that are off-limits for any scheduling conflicts. Jacquelyn Strickland, a licensed professional counselor, has developed a program for parents and adolescents called "Building Family Bridges." All families meet and share a meal at the beginning of each of the nine weekly sessions. During this mealtime together, participants are presented a mealtime discussion starter. This activity models how healthy families make time to eat together, and demonstrates that this can be an excellent time for meaningful discussion. Jacquelyn also structures this activity into her own family to really find out what is going on with her own sons, ages 15 and 18.

Discussion starters may range from "Share what you are most grateful for this week" to "One difficulty I am having that I would like support for is...' It's also a good idea to let family members take turns in creating discussion starters.

And do you know what's amazing? Chatting and chewing becomes some of the most important time spent together during the session. Jacquelyn reports that before this, many families never ate together, much less had conversations of any significance during those times.

Your church could provide opportunities like this too!

2. Make interactions with parents and kids nonthreatening. Dave McClellan, former director of student ministries at The Chapel in Akron, Ohio, maps out an easy process for kids and

parents to build relationships:
- Get families in the same room.
- Get parents interacting with kids other than their own.
- Get parents interacting with their own kids.

3. Provide training and resources. More and more companies are publishing helps for families. For example, Group Publishing produced a project that helps churches equip families for a family devotion time. Joani wrote *Fun Excuses to Talk About God* as a way to bring fun, creative, and relational devotional material into homes. In addition to the book for parents, Joani produced a four-session, church-led discussion guide. Families come together at church to learn how to conduct family devotions in an unforgettable way. (The sessions make for great family time at church, but can be done with parents only.) Families can experiment during the week and bring back questions, ideas, and support for one another. The books use all the educational techniques that we believe make a long-lasting faith impact.

4. Help parents be alert to "teachable moments." When families put up their "God antennae," it's amazing what they can teach! For example, empower parents to use the media as a teaching tool. If someone on the screen uses foul language, engages in violence to solve a problem, or gets involved sexually with someone other than his or her spouse—use these examples to teach Christian values. Say, "That's not the kind of language we use in our family." Or "Our family doesn't resort to violence to solve problems—we talk it out." Or "We believe God invented marriage as a special relationship." Instead of letting the media run rampant without discussion, turn it around to open up topic discussions.

5. Help parents just "be" with their kids. Royce Frazier, a Kansas marriage and family therapist, says he helps parents "let go" and simply be present with their children without an agenda.

Now doesn't that sound freeing? He's found that when parents stop trying so hard, they actually are more successful in relating to each other and to their children! Ahh...

6. Help parents realize their families don't have to be perfect. Often there's a false perception that "Christian" families don't have problems—they're perfect. Not true. Just page through Scripture and see for yourself. We can help families see that God's grace is sufficient for families today as it was in the Bible. Tim Smith, family minister at Calvary Community Church in Westlake Village, California, recently taught a ten-week series called, "So You Thought Your Family Was Messed Up!" Every week the group explored Bible families who dealt with ten timeless issues. For instance, "Abraham's Move to the West Coast" dealt with a mobile society; "Lot's Last Night in Sodom" covered sexual identity, homosexuality, and same-sex marriage; "Ishmael's Single Mom" talked about single parenting; "Joseph's Wild Dreams" explored rivalries and jealousies; and "Joseph's Family Recovery" dealt with family healing. You get the idea. Making the Bible relevant for families makes roots go deep.

7. Help families see the sacred in the ordinary. David Thomas points out that families are living "holy moments" all the time—they just don't recognize it. What would happen if families would attach "God thoughts" to their day-to-day activities? What if bathing a child reminded the family of his or her baptism? What if eating a meal together could connect with the Lord's Supper? What if communicating with each other were a reminder of the gift of prayer?

Royce Frazier tells about a favorite tradition his family celebrates near Easter. They share a Passover meal. As they remember the Israelites' deliverance from Egypt, they too recall "near death" experiences that happened in the past. They celebrate the times the Angel of Death passed over their family. Miraculously, each child in the family has lived through a dangerous event that they retell each Passover. It's an incredible way for the Frazier family to give thanks for God's abundant grace and goodness.

Families are fertile soil for long-term, deep faith impact. Take advantage of this learning environment as you help roots go deep.

"A good education is the next best thing to a pushy mother."

CHARLES SCHULZ

REFERENCES

1. Ben Freudenburg with Rick Lawrence, *The Family-Friendly Church* (Loveland, CO: Group Publishing, 1998), 10.

2. *Effective Christian Education: A National Study of Protestant Congregations, A Six-denomination Report,* (Minneapolis, MN: Search Institute, 1990), 41.

3. Nancy Leffert, Peter L. Benson, and Jolene L. Roehlkepartain, *Starting Out Right: Developmental Assets for Children* (Minneapolis, MN: Search Institute, 1997), 24-25.

4. David M. Thomas, "Family Comes of Age in the Catholic Church," Journal of Family Ministry (Summer 1998), 49-50.

5. Freudenburg and Lawrence, *The Family-Friendly Church*, 28.

6. Soledad O'Brien, "Dream Home 2000," USA Weekend (April 3-5, 1998), 6.

7. George Barna, "News Release: Churches Have Opportunity to Help Parents." (Oxnard, CA: Barna Research Group, Ltd., January 15, 1998).

Falling Among Thorns

"Other seed fell among thorns,
which grew up and choked the plants,
so that they did not bear grain.

[They], like seed sown among thorns,
hear the word;
but the worries of this life,
the deceitfulness of wealth
and the desires for other things
come in and choke the word,
making it unfruitful."

MARK 4:7, 18-19

Weeds. It seems they've been around since that dreaded sinful day in the Garden of Eden. Weeds were obviously a part of everyday life in Jesus' time. His followers understood the problems weeds posed.

The thorny weeds Jesus described deprive a crop of life-giving sunshine. Their fast-growing roots suck away precious water. They abduct the nutrients from the soil.

But Jesus' story takes an interesting twist on the role of the weeds. In Jesus' explanation of the parable, the weeds are not depicted as completely external adversaries. Look carefully at Mark 4:19. Those who hear the Word are not ultimately defeated by a frontal attack from an outside enemy. They're defeated by their own distractions. Their own responses make them unfruitful—their worrying, their giving in to the deceitfulness of wealth, their desires for other things.

Weeds pose a problem of stealth. Sometimes they appear innocent, growing so subtly that a person may not realize their choking potential.

What's at work in our churches that may be choking the Word? Could it be that these weeds are so subtle that we aren't aware of their danger? Is it possible that worries, deceitfulness of wealth, and desires for other things could be surreptitiously distracting our learners?

We believe there's ample evidence that weeds are indeed flourishing in the church's fields.

Cleaning the Fields

Farmer Bud knows how insidious weeds can be. For years he's battled the sinister "creepin' jenny," a long vine-like weed. "Some years I had to cultivate the field four times to get rid of that stuff," he says. Weeds are like that. They can be very resilient and tough to eradicate.

Bud knows he must be on guard at all times. If ever he gets complacent, the weeds will take over. Once they get a foothold, they can quickly rage out of control. "Like the cockleburs around here," Bud says, shaking his head in utter disgust. "If they aren't killed, they'll reproduce into many more. Then you've got a real problem."

The dangers described by Jesus are similar. If noxious distractions aren't controlled early, they'll quickly get out of control. When worries and unhealthy desires flourish, hearers of the Word will not bear fruit.

The danger of weeds is a big deal for Bud. Many times we've ridden with him along the county roads that slice through the South Dakota plains. He carefully scans every farmer's fields. Whenever he spots a field pimpled with thorny weeds, his upper lip curls and his head begins to slowly shake. "Look at that. What a shame! They spend all that money on good seed, and then they let their fields go. And they wonder why their yields are down! Some people just don't care. They just get by."

In the fields we farm in the church, it's time to start up the tractor. It's time to cultivate. It's time to rid the fields of those thorny weeds.

The Danger of Rewards, Bribes, and Competition

Many readers breeze by the thorny part of the Parable of the Sower. They read about "the worries of this life, the deceitfulness of wealth and the desires for other things," and they dismiss these as commonly mentioned millstones.

But wait. Jesus is not simply listing problems here. He's pleading with us to understand the relationship between these things and the learning and application of his Word. He's trying to awaken us to the subtle things that can sneak in and short-circuit the learning process.

Have these subtle influences infiltrated the church? Have some weeds grown so gradually for so long that we either don't notice them or we've come to believe they're not really weeds at all? We believe it's time to take a sobering look at some thorny weeds growing right under our noses.

Game Show Greed

We recently visited a church with a large Sunday morning children's program. Peppy music played as some two hundred kids streamed into the colorfully decorated children's center. A professional-looking stage was the focal point. The kids quickly moved to the four color-coded sections of seating. Each child seemed to know where to report.

Then the bright theatrical lighting flooded the stage. And the host, a young man in a colorful suit, bounded onto the stage while the band pumped out a loud fanfare. "Hey, kids!" he shouted into his wireless microphone. "Remember, the section out there who behaves the best gets two extra Bible Bucks per person! Now, who brought a new friend this morning?" Several kids raised their hands. "Awesome! Ushers, give them each five Bible Bucks!" The rewarded kids snatched the green currency and immediately counted the bills to make sure they got their due. Meanwhile the guests they brought looked on in bewilderment.

"Now it's time for Bible Memory Mania!" The young crowd cheered. "Here's how it works. The person who's memorized the most verses from this month's book of the Bible will win one hundred Bible Bucks! That's right, one hundred Bible Bucks! OK, you know this month's assignment is Psalm 74. Who memorized at least one verse?" Dozens of hands went up. "Great! Who memorized at least five verses?" Several hands shot up. "Super! Anybody memorize ten or more?" One small girl in the front row raised her hand.

"Rachel, you memorized at least ten verses this week? Come up here on stage," beckoned the host. The slight-framed girl shyly stepped onto the big stage. She shaded her eyes from the glare of the spotlights. The host asked, "How much of Psalm 74 did you memorize?"

"Well, I know the whole psalm," Rachel muttered.

"The whole psalm?!" the host exclaimed. "Let's see, that's twenty-three verses! You memorized twenty-three verses?"

"Yes."

"Well, can you recite them for us?"

And then, while the host held the microphone, little Rachel began: "O God, why hast thou cast us off forever? Why doth thine anger smoke against the sheep of thy pasture? Remember. . ." On and on she went. With hardly any hesitation she recited and recited and recited in almost robotic fashion. Several minutes later she indeed finished the psalm—all twenty-three verses. Everyone in the room was amazed. The host squealed, "Rachel! That was incredible! Congratulations! You've earned the one hundred Bible Bucks this morning!" Rachel politely grasped the wad of bills and returned to her seat.

"Next week we'll have another one hundred Bible Bucks to give away," the host shouted. "Let's see who can beat Rachel!"

At the end of the hour, the kids were released to visit the "Salvation Store"—a clever shop filled with mountains of candies, toys, trinkets, and tokens. Signs prominently marked the price of each item—in Bible Bucks. In a gold-rush-like frenzy the kids elbowed one another to redeem their Bible Bucks for the colorful treasures.

What were these kids learning? The Parable of the Sower haunted us. Was this program a thorny example of unhealthy distractions? The intentions were good. But did the program actually enhance the "deceitfulness of wealth" and "the desires for other things"? What was the real focus? What will these kids remember? Could the rush for Bible Bucks indeed choke the Word?

"Paid" Attention

Many churches have systems of rewards and/or punishments that supposedly encourage confirmation students and other young teenagers to attend the adult worship services. Church leaders desire that young people get in the habit of attending church and listening carefully to the pastor's sermons.

A church in Arizona devised an incentive program that lures teenagers with real cash. Each week the youth are handed fill-in-the-blank sermon worksheets. They need to pay attention to the sermons to write in the specific answers the pastor has in mind.

At the end of each quarter, the students' worksheets are compiled and graded. Kids who turn in at least ten weeks worth of completed worksheets receive $10 in cash.

Is this the best way to help kids fall in love with God's Word? Or is this another distraction of "desires for other things" that Jesus is trying to warn us against? Do such pay-for-attendance programs really produce the kind of fruit God wants?

Many churches struggle with confirmation, baptism, and new member classes for young people. Again, intentions are good, but results often indicate we've woefully lost sight of the goal. When these programs are applied, many churches see an exodus of young people—both a physical exodus and a spiritual exodus. This phenomenon was documented recently in a denominational magazine. Rich Melheim of Stillwater, Minnesota, responded with a letter to the magazine:

> My best guess on why they don't come back is that they were never there. Their bodies might have been there, but their hearts and minds were somewhere else. Until we decide to concentrate more on faith formation than information, on filling in the blanks in lives more than filling in the blanks in workbooks, and on creating a context of love for the content of the gospel, my guess is that the...church will continue to have a three-fourths dropout rate.[1]

THE PROBLEM WITH BRIBES

Churches have used reward programs for so long that few people question their ultimate effectiveness or their possible weedy effect on learners' long-term fruit-bearing. These programs have reached sacred cow status. Because of that, some people's defensiveness unfurls into full battle mode. But we ask you to stick with us and explore this sensitive issue with a fresh perspective.

What many call "rewards" are in fact bribes. Yes, we understand this is an uglier term. But it seems to more aptly fit church scenarios such as those described above. A bribe is usually an unrelated goody that is offered to coerce people into doing something they wouldn't ordinarily do. A bribe is a distraction. The briber says, "Keep your eye on this tempting goody while you do for me what you don't want to do."

This psychology is called behaviorism, popularized by psychologist B. F. Skinner.

He conducted most of his research on rodents and pigeons, and then applied what he learned to the human species. His work centered around the idea of "do this and you'll get that." Dogs can be trained to sit up if they're rewarded with a treat. A bird trapped in a box can be trained to peck at a certain spot if seeds then drop into a dish. A little girl can be trained to memorize King James text if she gets one hundred Bible Bucks.

Skinner's concept has been widely accepted. "Do-this-and-you'll-get-that" thinking is practiced by dog trainers, teachers, parents, employers, lawmakers, and crooks. Preachers promise extra blessings if parishioners will drop more money into the offering plate. "Do this and you'll get that." Parents offer money for their children's good grades, extra hours of television for cleaning their rooms, lunch at McDonald's for enduring Sunday school. "Do this and you'll get that."

And Sunday school teachers offer all sorts of bribes: a gold star for showing up, a bookmark for bringing a Bible, a sticker for completing a worksheet, a ribbon for memorizing a verse, a candy bar for being docile. "Do this and you'll get that."

So, what's the problem? Aren't these examples simply "positive reinforcement"? Here's what the Parable of the Sower is telling us about "do this and you'll get that":

People focus more on the "that" than the "this."

They're distracted from the real issue. What the parable calls "desires for other things" may seem innocent enough. But when they distract a learner from the Word itself, they become choking weeds. These rewards become the focal point, not the Word.

Rewards play right into the parable's warning about "the deceitfulness of wealth." We know from other biblical teachings that wealth itself is not evil. But the deceitfulness comes in when the wealth becomes our overriding desire. It takes our eyes off what's really important. The deceitfulness then becomes a thorny weed, choking the Word and making it unfruitful.

Again, we know church people use rewards or bribes with good intentions. We often hear teachers say, "Listen, I just want my kids to know the Word. I'll do anything that works." But do bribes really work?

From a behaviorist's point of view, yes, they work. You can train an animal or a human to do certain things to get a treat. But what's really being learned? What fruit is being produced? Sadly, even a behaviorist will tell you that a bribed person is only being trained to perform for the bribe.

This isn't the kind of fruit God has in mind. He wants his children to have a deep relationship with him. Like any parent, he doesn't want that relationship based on goodies. He wants a relationship based on love, not on bribes. No parent wants to hear, "I'll tolerate you if you give me money every morning." Parents, including the Father in heaven, want a relationship built on unconditional love. Parents want to hear a child say, "I love you. I want a forever relationship with you. I love you because I love you, not because I expect goodies in return." Focusing on those goodies distracts the child from a genuine relationship.

That distracting focus can become addictive. Bribes are like dangerous drugs. The more they're used, the more they seem to be needed. Church-based reward systems can quickly get out of control—like weeds in a farmer's field.

A SHORTSIGHTED SOLUTION

Bribes can indeed elicit certain behaviors. But because the focus is on the bribe, the behaviors are often short-lived. Just as with a trained seal, when you stop feeding the treats, the desired behavior stops.

When we base Christian education programs on bribes, we're not building long-term habits. We're forcing short-term reactions based on what the parable calls "desires for other things." They're short-term because the motivation is induced from outside the learners—extrinsic motivation.

Our son, Matt, is currently really interested in aviation. He reads everything he can find on airplanes, airports, and air traffic control procedures. He digs out his dad's old aeronautical charts and devises mock flight plans across the country. He loves aviation!

But his friend Mark is another story. Mark has no interest in airplanes. Even when Matt tries to tempt him with his computer flight simulator, Mark just yawns.

Now, if the science teacher decides to teach a unit on aviation, who will fare better—Matt or Mark? What if the teacher offers extra points (extrinsic motivation) to students who submit an extra-credit aviation project? Who would be more motivated to tackle the project? Matt would jump at the chance! Not because he lusts for the bribe of the extra credit, but because he'd be intrinsically motivated.

Intrinsic motivation is preferable—and more powerful—than extrinsic motivation. Extrinsic motivation works only long enough for the learner to grab the goody. Then interest typically evaporates until another goody is dangled.

> "Knowledge which is acquired under compulsion
> obtains no hold on the mind."
>
> PLATO

REWARDS THAT CHOKE INTEREST

Not only are rewards distracting and shortsighted, they may also actually kill interest in the very things we want learners to learn. How could this be? Everyone understands the nature of bribes. They're designed to lure us into something we wouldn't normally find that attractive. Your parents probably taught you this. "Now, honey, if you'll eat your spinach, you can have dessert." After hearing things like this for years, you've figured it out—spinach is yucky and dessert is good.

So now whenever anyone tells you, "Do this and you'll get that," you already know that the "this" is yucky. It's spinach. It's not supposed to be desirable. If it were good like dessert, you wouldn't be asked to eat your spinach first. Rewards are distractions because they devalue the real thing.

Alfie Kohn reports on a number of research projects that support this contention in his book *Punished by Rewards*. In one such study, schoolchildren were split into two groups. The first group was told that to draw with felt-tip pens they must first draw with crayons. The other group was told the reverse. Two weeks later researchers found that whichever activity had been the prerequisite for the other was now less appealing to the students. Half the class didn't want to draw with felt-tip markers, and half avoided the crayons. Whatever was required to earn the bribe was devalued.[2]

Extrinsic rewards reduce intrinsic motivation. If a child's Sunday school teacher requires learning the Bible in order to get a goody, then the Bible must be distasteful. Just like spinach. Is that what we want?

Rewards and Cheating

Rewards distract. Sometimes this distraction can be so powerful as to cause covetousness and dishonesty. It's the "deceitfulness of wealth" described in the parable.

A Purdue University study found that 70 percent of teenage boys and 57 percent of girls felt that at least half their teammates would cheat in sports to gain points. Interestingly, the coach plays a significant role in players' decisions to cheat. Up to 70 percent of boys and 83 percent of girls said the coach had the most influence on whether they'd break the rules.

Researcher Joan L. Duda said, "Kids are more likely to do things that are illegitimate or injurious when the punishments are minor and the rewards in terms of accolades are great."[3]

We've observed children and youth "bend the rules" and cheat in church award programs, just to achieve their short-term goals of winning the goodies. Once again, this underlines the wisdom of the Parable of the Sower. The "desires for other things" can choke the Word.

Here's a story from one of our co-workers, Mikal Keefer, who works with children at his church:

I was leading games at our church's children's midweek program. One of the games involved having four groups of children doing a four-way Tug of War with a rope that was tied in a circle. The groups of kids took this game very seriously, tugging away with all their might. Each team pulled toward its own goal—a beanbag on the floor. The first team to reach the beanbag without letting go of the rope won.

As you might imagine, there was a lot of action, with teams cheering and groups of tug-of-warriors straining.

After one round, a little guy from one of the teams approached me with a sheepish look on his face. He said, "I don't think we should have won that last round, because I cheated." I was stunned, and asked him what he meant. "Well, I got the beanbag, but I sort of let go of the rope to do it."

During the year, I knew some kids had cheated. But with me as the solo referee and seventy-five kids roaring around the gym, I seldom actually saw anyone bending the rules.

And I hadn't seen this boy cheat. Neither had anyone else. He was turning himself in—the best example of sportsmanship and Christian character I had seen all year.

So I asked everyone to sit down in a circle, including the other adult leaders who were in the gym area. I said, "Have you ever been playing a game and trying your best, and because you were trying so hard to win you skipped a step, or missed a base, or broke a rule? You didn't mean to cheat...it just sort of happened. Turn to a partner and tell about a time that happened for you."

After the kids shared, I told them about a time I'd been playing softball and hit a home run. Except when I was racing around the bases I forgot to tag third base. I didn't want to turn around to touch the base, so I kept going. Nobody noticed...but I knew. And I didn't turn myself in.

I told the kids what had happened and gave a rousing affirmation to the boy who'd had the courage to do what I'd been too afraid and too proud to do when I was his age.

Then we went back to playing games.

An adult leader slid up next to me and said, "I think we should give this boy an extra twenty award bucks for being so honest."

I said that would be the worst thing to do—because in life you're seldom rewarded for being honest. Honest people pay more taxes. They return found wallets. Besides, this guy had just been rewarded in a far more enduring way, and had been held up as an example of Christlike behavior.

As the kids lined up to go out, I was still feeling great about having grabbed the teachable moment...until I saw the boy pass by me. He was showing off a fresh $20 award bill. The adult I'd talked with just couldn't resist offering an extrinsic reward—and that cheapened the entire experience.

Now, for our kids, honesty was about being rewarded, not being Christlike.

Was that adult volunteer well-intentioned? Yes. Was she wrong? Absolutely.

REWARDS IN THE REAL WORLD

Some church educators justify the use of rewards by alluding to the world of employment. "Rewards are a natural part of life," they say. "A worker puts in a day's work for day's pay." That's true. But a couple of things preclude that axiom from transferring to the world of learning in the church.

First, even in the employment world, many studies have shown that most people are not chiefly motivated on the job by money. Other more intrinsic factors motivate most workers—things such as job fulfillment, mission, sense of purpose, camaraderie with fellow workers.

Second, the process of growing closer to God is not an employment issue. Faith is not a nine-to-five job. It's a relationship of love with the Almighty. It cheapens the relationship to think of it as an exchange of goods and services.

JESUS AND REWARDS

Did Jesus attempt to motivate his followers with extrinsic rewards? Did he use bribes? Well, at the end of the Beatitudes he said, "Rejoice and be glad, because great is your reward in heaven" (Matthew 5:12a). But does that sound like the bribes we just discussed—do this and get a Bible Buck?

Did Jesus lure his people with goodies? Can you imagine him saying the following?

● If you do unto others what you want them to do to you, you get a lollipop!

 ● If you forgive more than seventy times seven, you get a gold star!

 ● If you love the Lord your God, you get a ribbon!

 ● If you love your neighbor as yourself, you get a dollar!

 ● If you feed my sheep, you get a trip to the zoo!

 ● If you go therefore and teach all nations, you get Twinkies!

Jesus didn't use bribes. Yet people throughout the ages have been motivated to change their lives as a result of his teaching. Somehow he was able to plant seeds with great results—without resorting to bribe programs.

In fact, his teaching emphasized the grace-oriented concept of giving without expecting anything in return. Look at Matthew 5:43-47:

> "You have heard that it was said, 'Love your neighbor and hate your enemy.' But I tell you: Love your enemies and pray for

those who persecute you, that you may be sons of your Father in heaven. He causes his sun to rise on the evil and the good, and sends rain on the righteous and the unrighteous. If you love those who love you, what reward will you get? Are not even the tax collectors doing that? And if you greet only your brothers, what are you doing more than others? Do not even pagans do that?"

Jesus asks us to give and give without expecting any reward here and now. Our reward is not earthly.

The author of Colossians writes: "Whatever you do, work at it with all your heart, as working for the Lord, not for men, since you know that you will receive an inheritance from the Lord as a reward" (Colossians 3:23-24a). Many people focus on the word *reward*, thinking this is a form of payment for services rendered. But the emphasis really belongs on the word *inheritance*.

Philip Kenneson and James Street, authors of *Selling Out the Church*, explain: "Most of us realize that an inheritance is more like a gift given than a reward earned, since we had little control over who our family was. Similarly, if God has graciously given us new life and adopted us into the household of God, the inheritance that goes with that privilege is not so much our birthright as a freely given gift."[4]

Beyond Rewards

Well-intentioned church people love to give gifts to their learners. That's one of the reasons rewards have become so commonplace. It's fun to give. And in many cases, it's quite appropriate to give gifts to learners.

How can we give gifts without proliferating the thorny weeds of rewards? We find some guidance in that passage in Colossians. Treat gifts more like inheritances. That removes the stigma of "do this and you'll get that." Avoid bribing learners with the distractions of rewards. But do take the opportunity to celebrate with learners.

From time to time, surprise your learners with treats, goodies, and gifts. Make it an unexpected bonus rather than an owed carrot on a stick. Focus on the biblical concept of grace rather than on the behavioral psychology of B. F. Skinner.

Move away from extrinsic motivation to intrinsic motivation. Retool your approach so that learners want to come, want to learn, desire to continue learning and growing after they leave you, and develop a lifelong hunger for God's Word—all without the need for any bribes. We'll look at some strategies to accomplish this in the next two chapters.

COMPETITION: TROPHIES FOR TRIVIA

Some churches have built an elaborate system of competition and awards around what's called Bible quizzing. Youth and children pore over the Scriptures in preparation for quiz meets where they compete in teams against adversaries from other churches. The winners get trophies and earn the opportunity to advance to the finals.

We observed one of these competitions in Colorado. Four-person teams of middle school students sat behind long tables with their hands poised on game-show buzzers. The very serious host read detailed questions related to Old Testament Scriptures. A sample:

"In the plagues against Pharaoh, what grains were not destroyed by the hail storm: 1) wheat and barley, 2) barley and flax, 3) wheat and spelt, 4) barley and spelt."

The kids furrowed their brows. A girl finally buzzed in with "wheat and spelt." She was correct, and her team went on to win the competition. We asked her later about the significance of the wheat and spelt question. She said, "Well, it's one of the plagues. It doesn't really mean a lot to me, other than it's God's Word. But it really doesn't mean that much."

"How will you use this information?" we asked.

"I don't know," she replied.

As we watched the winning and losing teams after the match, we noticed one girl who had performed quite well during the competition. But her team lost. She ran to her father and burst into tears. "I'm sorry, I'm sorry," she sobbed. "I wish we never would have come! I feel like such a loser."

This is the world of Bible quizzing. Is this really the best possible use of learners' time?

Once again, the church leaders who organize and administrate such activities have the best of intentions. They're trying to encourage Bible study by engaging kids in what they hope will be the thrill of competition. And these activities have gone on for so long, nobody questions their validity. But perhaps it's time to take a closer look.

What's the hidden curriculum here? What messages are really being communicated? We see a number of disturbing factors:

● **An emphasis on trivia.** To make the competitive bouts challenging, the organizers must write questions centering around rather obscure Bible facts. They can't include questions on larger, more significant matters such as Jesus' two great commandments. Too many students would know the answer. So the quizzing tends to concentrate on things such as wheat and spelt. What message does that send to students? Does the quizmaster's preoccupation with minutia communicate that the Bible's real use is as an encyclopedia of trivia? Does this perpetuate the bias that the Bible is not to be understood but merely jostled in short-term memory?

- **An emphasis on bribes.** The lures are the trophies, the temporary fame, the advancement to finals. Are these kids learning to love the Bible or learning to lust after the prizes?

- **A cauldron of worry.** The atmosphere at a Bible quizzing competition is often a pressure cooker of fretting and tension. When the competitors take their seats, all smiles disappear. This is serious business. That quizmaster wants to know about wheat and spelt and other fact-intensive subjects. We return to the Parable of the Sower. They "hear the word, but the worries of this life...choke the word." Competitive conflicts such as these promote worry. Does that contribute to the fruitfulness of the Word?

- **An adversarial relationship.** The whole concept of Bible quizzing hinges on competition. And competition relies on winners and losers. This setup naturally pits teams against one another. When it comes to Bible knowledge, Team A is hoping and praying that Team B knows fewer facts. Team A's glee is contingent upon Team B's failure. Is that what the church is all about—hoping someone else knows less of God's Word?

Let's examine these factors a little closer.

INCENTIVES FOR INCIDENTALS

Competitive Bible activities focus on the easily measurable. Whether it's Bible quizzing or memorization contests or timed fact look-up races, the criteria need to be concretely judged. That, by its nature, eliminates any broad inquiry that might require interpretive thought or life application.

The rules of such competition usually necessitate nit-picking. The wheat and spelt question is an example. In Bible memorization contests, competitors may lose if they say "said" instead of "sayeth." The prizes go to those who recall the minutia, not to those who understand the Word and apply it to their lives. What are children learning from such emphases?

Look at the teaching ministry of Jesus. How much time did he spend drilling his followers on minutia? Did he ever say anything like, "OK, folks, the first one to name the twelve tribes of Israel wins a camel saddle"? No, Jesus did not appear the least bit interested in spending time on trivial facts. He saw his mission far too urgent for that. He devoted his time to planting seeds that would bear fruit, that would lead to people coming into a loving relationship with him and his Father.

Is our mission any less urgent? Can we really afford the time to chase little facts, even if they are easy to measure?

"THE WORRIES OF THIS LIFE"

Competitive Bible activities breed tension and worry. It's the kind of tension and worry that diverts attention and suppresses positive learning.

This type of worry is akin to the worry generated by students facing academic examinations. Some people become mentally crippled when taking a test. Their worry causes them to perform poorly. Daniel Goleman writes about worry research in *Emotional Intelligence*:

> The number of worries that people report while taking a test directly predicts how poorly they will do on it.[5] The mental resources expended on one cognitive task—the worrying—simply

detract from the resources available for processing other information; if we are preoccupied by worries that we're going to flunk the test we're taking, we have that much less attention to expend on figuring out the answers. Our worries become self-fulfilling prophecies, propelling us toward the very disaster they predict.[6]

Contemporary researchers are now discovering the detrimental effects of worry on learning. But Jesus had this phenomenon nailed in the Parable of the Sower. "The worries of this life...choke the word." Think of competitive worries as thorny weeds that stunt the growth of the good plants. In the church we don't need to perpetuate competitive systems that create worry.

> *"Anxiety arises out of the interpersonal isolation*
> *and alienation from others that inheres in a pattern*
> *in which self-validation depends on triumphing over others."*
>
> ROLLO MAY, PSYCHOANALYST

LOOKING FOR LOSERS

Competitive activities have a core problem. They, by their nature, require losers. Educator Alfie Kohn writes in his book *No Contest:* "To say that an activity is structurally competitive is to say that it is characterized by what I call *mutually exclusive goal attainment*...This means, very simply, that my success requires your failure."[7]

Think about that a minute. If I want to play a competitive game of chess, I need you. If I want to do well, my goal is to win. If I want to win, I need you to lose. I can't succeed unless you fail. My joy depends upon your pain.

If you want to play a game of Bible Trivia, you need me. If you want to win the prize offered by your church, your goal is to win. If you want to win, you need me to know fewer Bible facts than you. You can't succeed unless I foul up. Your victory depends upon my defeat.

Is this the best way to approach learning in the church? Must we support a learning system that requires losers? What underlying messages are we really sending?

We noticed this brief news story in the July 19-21, 1996, edition of USA Today:

BIBLE CONTEST SLAYING: A Dadeville, Ala., man who was angry that he lost a Bible-quoting contest killed the man who bested him, police said. Gabel Taylor, 38, was shot once in the face. The name of the suspect was withheld.

Of course this is an extreme example. But it's the extreme end of the same competitive tension that exists in many churches' competitive Bible activities. If you endorse Bible memory competitions or Bible quizzing, it's not likely your competitors will shoot one another. But it is quite likely some will feel antagonistic toward the victors. Then the question becomes: Must churches engage in activities that engender antagonism toward other Christians in the pursuit of Bible knowledge and spiritual growth?

"Each one should test his own actions.
Then he can take pride in himself,
without comparing himself to somebody else,
for each one should carry his own load."

GALATIANS 6:4-5

A NATURAL PART OF LIFE?

Many church people condone competitive Bible activities by arguing that competition is simply a part of life. "It's everywhere!" they proclaim. That's true. In our society competition is widespread. We find it in sports, in the workplace, on the highway, in politics, and in our schools.

Our schools have taken competition to curious heights. Take the bell curve, for example. This system of grading places students on a bell-shaped curve. It requires that most students fall into the middle—"average performers." It also requires that a few students receive high grades. And it mandates that some students emerge as poor performers. The classroom records should show that most students receive B's and Cs', a few get A's and a few get D's and F's.

This system depends on competition, on pitting student against student. As in all competition, it requires losers. If learning is the goal, is it absolutely necessary that some people lose?

But church competition enthusiasts seem to find it irresistible to emulate the public schools and the secular society. "Kids are going to face competition out there in the world, so they might as well learn to deal with it," they say. Is that really the purpose of Christian education programs? To teach people how to beat one another?

"The notion that competition is necessary and useful
for kids to learn is exactly as sensible as saying:
'You know, there are a lot of carcinogens in the environment,
so we better start exposing kids to cancer-causing agents
as young as possible.'"

ALFIE KOHN, *NO CONTEST*

Yes, competition exists in our society. But not everything that exists in society needs to be adopted as a learning technique in our churches. We're about planting seeds of faith. Our goal centers around seeing those seeds germinate, grow, and bear fruit. This isn't a game. We needn't go into it with the prerequisite that some of our people must lose. Yes, some will miss out on salvation. But the metaphor of competitive sports doesn't fit God's desires for his world. We read in 2 Peter 3:9b: "He (the Lord) is patient with you, not wanting anyone to perish, but everyone to come to repentance." God is not desiring that some lose.

THE BIBLE AND COMPETITION

The Apostle Paul uses a race metaphor in 1 Corinthians 9:24-27. And Old and New Testament writers use war and battle metaphors. But do any of these uses indicate we should pursue competitive Bible learning activities? Does the whole emphasis of God's Word indicate that our relationship with the Lord should be built on competitive systems? Let's consider some evidence.

COMPETITION says: "Other people are obstacles to my success."

GOD'S WORD says: "There should be no division in the body, but that its parts should have equal concern for each other" (1 Corinthians 12:25).

COMPETITION says: "If I'm good enough, I'll win the prize."

GOD'S WORD says: "For it is by grace you have been saved, through faith—and this not from yourselves, it is the gift of God—not by works, so that no one can boast" (Ephesians 2:8-9).

COMPETITION says:
"If I'm last, I'm a failure."

GOD'S WORD says: "If anyone wants to be first, he must be the very last, and the servant of all" (Mark 9:35b).

COMPETITION'S PLACE

We find it difficult to justify the use of competition to compel learners to study God's Word and grow closer to him. But we're not going so far as to say that competition should be avoided everywhere.

Some fun-based competitive games can be used effectively in the church with children, youth, and adults. If the goal is fun and community-building, some of these competitive games can work—provided players know the goal is fun. The church softball league can help build fellowship—if players remember that's the goal.

You may find acceptable places for competitive games in the life of the church. But making spiritual growth a game of competition is dangerous. Do you see the distinction? It's a matter of goal.

If we choose to play Monopoly as a family, that can generate an evening of fun—provided we all keep it in that spirit. But when it comes to feeding our family, we don't want our family members competing for dinner, to see who eats and who goes hungry.

The same is true when it comes to the Bread of Life. Using competition to see who gets the most spiritual food is a dangerous practice. It's a bit too reminiscent of Charles Darwin's survival-of-the-fittest theory.

FROM COMPETITION TO COOPERATION

If competition is dangerous in Christian education, is there an alternative? Yes, it's student cooperation. Rather than attempting to motivate by pitting learners against one another, we can help them learn through cooperating with one another.

Let's look at the motivation factors at work in both competition and cooperation. Competition's driving motivators are the appeal of victory and the offsetting fear of losing. The chief motivators in cooperation are accountability to others and the knowledge that others are depending on you.

That's a stark comparison. Think about the concept of the church. It was not created as an environment for individuals to conquer one another. It was designed as a community where people support one another, as in the body illustration in 1 Corinthians 12. In a competitive environment, the only stake others have in your performance is a desire to see you fail.

Susan Grover, a California children's director, tells the story of Joshua, a little boy with a big, kind heart. At his former church, Joshua never seemed to fit. He was known as a loner because he resisted that church's popular program of competition and rewards. Finally his parents decided to try something different. They brought Joshua to Susan's church. Here he transformed into an outgoing participant with lots of friends. What made the difference? Joshua's parents credit the cooperative environment at Susan's church. Children are encouraged to work together for common learning goals. They're placed in small groups where they talk about their faith. They pray for one another. They want to see each other succeed.

It's time for many churches to change their mind-set from competition to cooperation. This does not mean giving up any pizazz. Cooperation can be just as stimulating as competition, but without the unsavory side-effects. You can encourage Bible memory without creating winners and losers. Cooperative activities are outlined in the book *Making Scripture Memory Fun.*

And you can encourage cooperation through the games you select. Many competitive games can be adapted to make them co-operative. Take the old Rock, Paper, Scissors game for example. The competitive version of that game has players trying to conquer one another by flashing a hand signal that would be superior over their opponent's. The rock symbol crushes the scissors, the paper covers the rock, the scissors cuts the paper. But with a simple twist, you can have a lot of fun making this game cooperative. Simply tell players their objective is to *match* their partner's symbol. We've used this cooperative game with all ages. Much laughter and fun always result. And everyone's a winner.

You'll find additional cooperative game ideas in these books: *Everyone's-a-Winner Games for Children's Ministry, Fun & Easy Games,* and *"Let's Play!" Group Games for Preschoolers.*

Long-Term Effects

To summarize our discussion on the use of rewards, bribes, and competition in Christian education, we ask you to examine the long-term effects of such approaches. Sure, we may see some short-term effects that appear positive. Learners may be able to recite a verse. Competitors may scour the Scriptures looking for a Bible fact. But those results are usually short-term. Learners quickly forget data that doesn't make the leap into long-term memory.

What does get stored in long-term memory from programs based on extrinsic rewards, bribes, and competition? It's often the experiences related to the intense emotions of conquest, failure, and the quest for goodies. These emotions can indeed choke the Word, as related in the Parable of the Sower.

Unfortunately the damage from some of these well-intentioned programs can last a long time. Farmer Bud knows about the long-term negative effect of weeds. "Lots of weed seeds around here can sit in the ground for twenty years and then pop up and try to take over a field. We can never drop our guard."

"A teacher who is attempting to teach
without inspiring the pupil with a desire to learn
is hammering on a cold iron."

HORACE MANN

REFERENCES

1. Rich Melheim, "Class of '78," The Lutheran (July 1998), 56.

2. Alfie Kohn, *Punished by Rewards* (New York, NY: Houghton Mifflin Company, 1993), 77.

3. From a Purdue University study presented to the North American Society for Psychology of Sport and Physical Activity, reported in the Associated Press, June 28, 1998.

4. Philip D. Kenneson and James L. Street, *Selling Out the Church* (Nashville, TN: Abingdon, 1997), 55.

5. John Hunsley, "Internal Dialogue During Academic Examinations," Cognitive Therapy and Research (December 1987) as quoted in Daniel Goleman, *Emotional Intelligence* (New York, NY: Bantam Books, 1995), 84.

6. Goleman, *Emotional Intelligence*, 84.

7. Alfie Kohn, *No Contest* (New York, NY: Houghton Mifflin Company, 1992), 4.

CHAPTER EIGHT

LIFELONG LEARNING THROUGH INTRINSIC MOTIVATION

"The most important motive for work in the school
and in life is the pleasure in work,
pleasure in its result and the knowledge of the value
of the result to the community.
I have known children who
preferred schooltime to vacation."

ALBERT EINSTEIN

Bob, a Christian education director in Pennsylvania, dreamed up an idea he hoped would motivate his church's kids to memorize the books of the Bible. With great hoopla, he announced that he would shave his head if one hundred kids could accomplish the Bible memorization feat. Bob is well-liked by the children and adults at his church, so he had high confidence in his plan's success.

The campaign, though well publicized, started out slowly. By the first deadline, only five kids had learned the books of the Bible. So Bob graciously extended the deadline, and grew out his hair a bit longer to increase the students' anticipation. He built a big thermometer and placed it in the hall to motivate more kids to work on their memorization. After a while longer, the hall thermometer showed that only a handful of kids had memorized the books of the Bible.

But Bob's dream of one hundred kids just wasn't materializing. Most of the children were simply not interested in his project. So he turned to the adults in the congregation. He tried to motivate them to memorize the books of the Bible. He announced that for every two grown-ups who'd do the memory drill, he'd count them as one more point toward the goal of one hundred. Apparently he feared that if each adult counted as one, the goal would be too easily reached.

He didn't need to worry about that. The adults showed no more interest than the kids. The thermometer continued to shiver well down in hypothermal territory.

Finally Bob announced a new final deadline, goading the congregation to show up with cameras cocked, ready to record the big shave-off. On the designated Sunday morning, the parents brought their cameras, but the thermometer never budged. The children sat in the back staring blankly.

But Bob, showing tremendous grace, shaved his head anyway. And as the last hair dropped to the carpet, he issued another challenge—a candy bar to any child who'd learn just the books of the New Testament!

LEARNING WHEN THEY'RE READY TO LEARN

Bob is a wonderful, well-meaning guy. And he looks better with hair. But what happened here? Why was he unable to motivate those kids? Well, he made a very common but misplaced assumption about how learners are motivated. He thought he could motivate his learners into doing something they wouldn't ordinarily do themselves.

The truth is, we can't motivate learners. *We can only influence how they motivate themselves.* It's our job to create an environment for intrinsic motivation. Attempts at imposing motivation upon others simply do not work long-term.

Most of the kids in Bob's church felt no intrinsic motivation to learn the books of the Bible. They saw no value in the memory drill. And seeing a man get a haircut in exchange for a memory test didn't really connect with them. Even for those children who did complete the assignment, if their motivation centered more on Bob's baldness than the value of knowing the books of the Bible, they're not likely to retain the Bible's table of contents long-term. As the Parable of the Sower says, they had "desires for other things."

If rewards, bribes, and hairless leaders don't motivate learners to learn, what does? Intrinsic motivation—a self-driven quest to change and grow.

Think for a moment about yourself. What is a subject you love, something in which you've really excelled? Perhaps it's cooking, or bicycling, or storytelling, or nuclear physics. How did you get so good at this? Did you excel because someone constantly diverted your attention to trinket prizes? Not likely. You accomplished your higher goals because you wanted to—to satisfy your own curiosity, to act on something you care about, to experience the joy of using your skill in the real world, to bask in the sheer joy of learning something that fascinates you.

That's intrinsic motivation. And it's more powerful and longer lasting than any extrinsic motivation scheme.

University of Chicago psychologist Mihaly Csikszentmihalyi followed two hundred art students for eighteen years after they left art school. He found that the students who pursued painting for the sheer joy of it went on to become serious painters. Those who were distracted in art school by desires for fame and wealth drifted away from art after graduating.[1]

Intrinsically motivated learners become immersed in their learning. This occurs when they operate in a state of readiness. They're best ready to learn when they're neither bored nor anxious.

No external force will hammer long-term learning into anyone's bored mind. You can teach and teach and teach, but if the students find the subject matter or your presentation style boring, you're wasting your time. They're not learning.

And as the Parable of the Sower and our previous chapter demonstrate, anxiety and worry tend to "choke the word, making it unfruitful." Coercing learners to win or threatening them with embarrassment will not produce long-term fruit.

People learn best when they're intrinsically motivated, when they want to learn. How can we create an environment that encourages self-motivation? The approach we call authentic learning relies on intrinsic motivation. Authentic learning's characteristics help learners want to learn.

Another way to say authentic is *real*. Let's use the acronym REAL to explore some of the characteristics of authentic learning.

R elational

E xperiential

A pplicable

L earner-based

R = RELATIONAL

What's the most common non-word in children's Sunday school classes? We believe it's "shhh." We've clocked some teachers and found this annoying sound occupying surprisingly large portions of their communication time with their students. Why? Somewhere along the line these teachers picked up the notion that classroom success is judged by student silence.

Millions of students receive the message in church that talking is misbehaving. Time after time they're scolded for speaking with one another, even if they're discussing the Bible topic. What's the hidden curriculum here? We fear students learn that God's Word is something you listen to others talk about, that faith is a lecturer's topic. It's no wonder most people have difficulty discussing their faith with peers. They're discouraged from doing so even in church.

Why do teachers insist on doing so much of the talking? Mostly, it's an issue of control. They believe the teacher's chief role is that of a warden or zoo keeper. If a church leader would visit their classroom and observe students talking, teachers fear they'd be accused of "allowing the monkeys to run the zoo."

The notion of setting aside time for learners to talk and work together is quite foreign to many church teachers. But the building of learner-to-learner relationships is one of the secrets of an authentic learning environment that encourages intrinsic motivation. Unfortunately, many teachers spend their time either separating students to keep them quiet or pitting them against one other in competitive contests. Those aren't the makings of a relational ministry.

Relational ministry devotes substantial time to positive learner-to-learner talk. Students in these settings hear not only what the teacher has to say, but what their peers have to say, and they have a chance to share their own thoughts. In a relational setting, the teacher is less a "sage on the stage" and more a "guide on the side." Rather than dispensing all the information, the relational teacher allows time for learners to share their thoughts with one another. Rather than always telling learners what a Bible story means, the relational teacher says, "Turn to a partner and tell how this story relates to your life."

Yes, this requires the teacher to relinquish total control. But it grants an element of control to the learners. Possession of some of the control in a learning situation contributes to learners' intrinsic motivation. People are more motivated to learn when they can "drive" part of the way with friends.

Gordon and Becki West took a group of fifth- and sixth-graders on a mission trip to an orphanage in Mexico. On prior trips, the adult leaders lectured these middle schoolers during the teaching time. But the Wests wanted to switch to a more relational style. So over the protests of the other adults, they asked the kids to discuss their learnings in small groups. "It'll be chaos!" the other adult sponsors warned. Gordon and Becki asked the kids tough questions, such as, "Why would God allow these Mexican kids to have so little when we have so much?" Much to the adult sponsors' surprise, these fifth- and sixth-graders delved deeply into the subject. They were highly self-motivated to learn about God's message for them.

In addition to enhanced learning, the relational approach builds friendships. People of any age form friendships through talking with one another. When we allow time for relationship-building, we also contribute to an authentic learning environment that encourages intrinsic motivation. If learners make and strengthen friendships at church, they're more motivated to come to church. And, incidentally, they're more motivated to bring new people to church—because it's a friendly, relational place.

We've noticed the strong bring-a-friend impact with Hands-On Bible Curriculum, which involves lots of student-to-student talk and activities. While Sunday school attendance nationwide is declining, 80 percent of the churches that have switched to this relational curriculum report their attendance is growing. Debbie, a Hands-On teacher in California, said, "The lessons have a way of introducing God's Word in a safe way. It works for tough, standoffish, too-cool kids. Once they're involved, they can't resist! The students get actively involved. The teachers get involved. A relationship is built where mutual things can happen. By the end of the class, these tough kids are the first to share prayer needs!"

Learner time spent talking and enjoying one another's company is not wasted time. It's time invested building an environment for intrinsic motivation.

Contrast these relational models with Bob's haircut campaign. His plan involved no student-to-student interaction, cooperation, or camaraderie. The environment was not conducive to intrinsic motivation.

On the other hand, Jesus modeled a relational ministry. His questions provoked lots of relational discussion among his learners. And he created relational environments when he combined ministry with mealtimes, such as with the feeding of the five thousand, the wedding at Cana, the meal with Zacchaeus, and the Last Supper. The learners in Jesus' ministry shared great intrinsic motivation to learn more from this relational teacher.

E = EXPERIENTIAL

Experiential learning—or active learning—encourages intrinsic motivation. That's because the experience fully *involves* the learner. Nobody is a passive observer.

What do you like to do? Bowl? Read novels? Swim? Talk on the phone? Did your interest in this activity blossom through listening to somebody lecture on the subject? Did you become intrigued by filling out a worksheet? It's doubtful. Your interest likely ignited when you actively tried these activities. You were intrinsically motivated because you got to learn by doing.

Experiential learning has the same effect with learning in the church. You'll encourage intrinsic motivation when you use active learning. People's interest and motivation increases when they're allowed to learn by doing, when multiple senses are involved. Learners need to see, hear, touch, taste, and smell what they're learning about.

Studies show that the intrinsically motivated students in active-learning situations learn and remember more than their passive-learning counterparts. Look at the results of the following research from the University of Indiana:

After 30 days, students remember:
10 % of what they hear
15% of what they see
20% of what they hear and see
40% of what they discuss
80% of what they do
90% of what they teach to others

In experiential learning situations, students enjoy the adventure of making discoveries. Their own discoveries. Learners are not viewed as empty vessels waiting to be filled by authority figures. They get to crawl into the subject, pursue nooks that interest them, ask questions, find out what works, make their own connections to the real world, and share their insights with fellow learners. That's motivating—intrinsically motivating.

Let's look back on our friend Bob and his books-of-the-Bible challenge. His drill lacked an experiential multi-sensory approach. He could have incorporated some active elements to his project and increased the intrinsic motivation. Instead of simply telling kids to memorize the books of the Bible, why not make the activity hands-on? He could have led sessions that allowed kids to make and label their own little tabs to attach to each book of their Bibles.

We used this approach in Group's Treasure Hunt Bible Adventure vacation Bible school. Here kids highlighted key verses in their Bibles. They made special tabs to attach near some verses. One tab was labeled "trust." Another was called "love." One of the key verses was John 17:20: "My prayer is not for them alone. I pray also for those who will believe in me through their message." Beside this verse the kids mounted a tab that bore their own fingerprints, as a reminder that Jesus is praying for them personally.

Kids loved this experiential Bible activity! They were certainly intrinsically motivated. By the end of the week, kids were asking questions such as, "Would it be OK if I mark other verses I like in my Bible?" One boy said he has a relative battling cancer. He said, "Next time I go see him I'm taking this Bible so I know how to find verses to help him."

That's intrinsic motivation—boosted by the use of experiential learning.

Jesus built a ministry around experiential learning. When he healed the paralytic, when he raised Lazarus from the dead, when he challenged the bystanders to cast the first stone at the woman caught in adultery, when he washed the disciples' feet—he encouraged intense intrinsic motivation among his learners.

A = APPLICABLE

Learners show a definite lack of motivation when they can't see how the information relates to their real lives. In our workshops we often ask everyone who ever took a biology class to stand. Then we ask them to remain standing if they remember a question we guarantee was on one of their biology tests. The question: What is the difference between meiosis and mitosis? The participants usually chuckle nervously. Then over 95 percent of them always sit down.

We're sure their biology teachers would be very disappointed. The schools spent a lot of time drilling students on the meaning of those two terms. They printed that question on final exams. What happened? Why are the long-term results of those biology classes so pitiful?

Very few students could see any life relevance in the meiosis/mitosis information. This is a classic illustration of how our brains sort data into short- and long-term bins. That bit of biology data was stored only long enough to help all those students pass a test. Then it was lost forever. The students in those classes lacked the intrinsic motivation to really learn and retain that information, because they saw no way to apply it to their real lives. Their teachers never demonstrated how the knowledge of meiosis and mitosis would make a speck of difference in their real lives.

When we attempt to drill Bible facts into our learner's brains without a vivid understanding of how that information applies to their lives, that data will go to the same short-term waste bin as meiosis and mitosis. There's no intrinsic motivation to learn it.

Here's another reason Bob's books-of-the-Bible exercise fizzled. He never demonstrated *why* his students should know the books of the Bible. That list of names seemed irrelevant and meaningless to them. They couldn't understand how it related to their everyday lives. The promise of a shave and haircut created neither the necessary extrinsic nor intrinsic motivation to change most of his students' behavior. He forgot about the importance of life application.

When we connect Bible lessons to learners' real world, we encourage their natural curiosity, which propels them to learn and retain. God never intended his Word to be treated like meiosis and mitosis. His Word is not a collection of facts to be temporarily memorized. His Word is a guide for how we should live today, for how we should know him, for how we should deepen our relationship with him. After all, God wants us to worship him, not his book.

When we approach the Bible as a relevant guide book for our contemporary lives, we open the window for intrinsic motivation. God provided his Word with application in mind. People of all ages, from all walks of life, will quickly find relevant help in the Bible, provided the teachers and the curriculum keep application in mind.

We like the example of Burton Visotzky, who leads a Bible study with high-powered CEOs in New York City. "We have learned over the years that Genesis and Exodus...are full of stories that afford opportunities for conversation about marriage, children, family, and community," he said. "And Genesis and Exodus are replete with tales that illustrate the moral questions that beset business folks on a daily basis."

Visotzky applied the story of Moses bargaining with Pharaoh to these executives' interest in negotiation. Visotzky piqued their interest with Moses' early negotiation tactic found in Exodus 5:1: "Let my people go, so that they may hold a festival to me in the desert." The teacher teased his CEO students with good questions: "All he could muster before mighty Pharaoh was a meek request for a three-day weekend? What kind of a wimp way was this to bargain, anyway?"

One of the Bible study participants, an advertising executive, replied, "He (Pharaoh) reacts, and that's good. Had Moses started with asking for the whole hog, Pharaoh would have thrown him out, maybe killed him. The fact that Pharaoh ups the work quota is just a negotiating strategy on his part. There's definitely movement here."[2]

That's making the Bible relevant to these students' everyday lives. They're eager to learn because they're intrinsically motivated.

Look also at the learning approach used by Jesus. His lessons emphasized life application at every turn. His ministry was not a tedious academic exercise in drilling facts. He never insisted his followers memorize terms such as meiosis and mitosis. Every teaching, every parable, every active-learning experience applied directly to people's lives. Thus his followers experienced intrinsic motivation to learn. And their lives were never the same.

We can follow Jesus' example. We must find ways to apply our lessons directly to our learners' lives. When we do, they'll be intrinsically motivated to learn. And their lives will be changed.

L = LEARNER-BASED

We provide an atmosphere for intrinsic motivation when we design our educational systems around the learners, not the teachers. It's obvious that learners will show more interest if the whole approach is customized for their benefit, their interests, their learning styles, their attention span.

We're devoted to this learner-based philosophy at Group Publishing. That's why, when developing new curriculum, the first people we talk with are the students. For example, every year when we begin development of a new vacation Bible school curriculum, we assemble children and ask their opinions on our ideas. They pretest every lesson, every craft, every snack, every song, every learning activity. They're brutally honest. We've had to start over many times because these pint-sized consultants told us we were off-track.

When you plan, do you start with your learners? We recently conducted a survey with Christian education directors around the country. We asked, "Who are the important people in your decisions when selecting a Sunday school curriculum?" No one mentioned the students. If we desire an atmosphere where intrinsic motivation thrives, we must remember the learners in our planning. We must be learner-based.

The whole issue of choice provides a good opportunity to explore the benefits of a learner-based environment. When we allow learners of any age to make choices about what they'll learn and how they'll learn, they'll feel more intrinsically motivated.

This is another way our friend Bob missed an opportunity. His books-of-the-Bible exercise allowed for no student choice. He made all the choices. He chose the assignment, how it should be done, when it should be done, how it would be assessed, and how it would be rewarded. The kids were passive spectators to Bob's choice-making. And thus they felt little intrinsic motivation.

When we allow learners to make choices, we show them a measure of respect. And they feel a sense of ownership in their learning. In addition, they learn more.

Many researchers have documented the educational value in granting elements of choice to students. Pittsburgh second-graders completed more learning tasks in less time when they were allowed to choose which tasks they would work on at any given time.[3]

Preschool children in Massachusetts were divided into two groups. The first group was given a stack of materials and told to create a collage. Members of the second group were allowed to choose their materials for their collages. The materials they could choose from were identical to those automatically given to the first group. The second group's work was judged to be far more creative than the first group's, even though both groups had the same materials with which to work.[4]

Two groups of college students were similarly followed in New York. The first group was assigned a problem to work. The second group was given the chance to pick a problem among several choices. The second group showed much more interest and involvement.[5]

The vacation Bible school programs we create allow the children to choose their roles for the week. They get to decide if they'd like to be a reader or a materials manager or a prayer person. And they make choices about crafts. They're encouraged to make them using their own creativity rather than trying to copy the teacher's craft. And they're never asked to pickle their brains on teacher-based VBS worksheets, which allow no creativity and no choice.

This is especially important with young children. Arthur Ellis and Jeffrey Fouts write in their book *Research on Educational Innovations:* "Researchers at the UCLA Medical Center have discovered that children below the age of 10 have brain activity that is unusually rich in the secretion of theta waves, thought to be associated with creativity. Whether in the future this knowledge will stop teachers from handing out worksheet after worksheet to these naturally creative little characters remains speculative."[6]

There's a side benefit to this learner-based approach of giving students opportunities to be creative and to make choices. There are fewer discipline problems. Since they're intrinsically motivated to learn, they're far less apt to cause problems.

Barbara McCombs and Jo Sue Whisler say it well in *The Learner-Centered Classroom and School:* "With a learner-centered approach, teachers report that there is less student disruption and fewer discipline problems...The point is, when educators put learners squarely in the center of the learning process, they do what works best for each student as an individual learner. The result is increased motivation, learning, and achievement."[7]

Jesus employed a learner-based approach. His repeated use of physical healing shows an intent to zero in on individuals' needs. He customized his methods for each type of audience. And he allowed the ultimate learner choice—the choice, the free will, to believe.

Making the Change

So, are you ready to move from extrinsic attempts at motivation to intrinsic motivation? We must caution you to apply realistic expectations to the change process. Don't expect learners (or teachers) to immediately cheer if you cut off the reward programs tomorrow. They may be quite addicted to the awards and bribes.

When you begin implementing more intrinsically motivated approaches, some will demonstrate their dependence on the extrinsic rewards. We've heard kids in such situations say, "If I do what you ask, what will I get for it?" It can be a slow, sometimes difficult process to wean students off their dependence on external rewards. But it's worth it. In fact, the more difficult this weaning process may be, the more important it is to undertake it.

These extrinsic "desires for other things" are described by Jesus as thorny weeds. It's always well worth our time to weed the field if we want to produce fruit.

REFERENCES

1. Daniel Goleman, *Emotional Intelligence* (New York, NY: Bantam Books, 1995), 93.

2. Burton Visotzky, "Bible in the Boardroom?" Inc. magazine (July 1998), 29-30.

3. Margaret C. Wang and Billie Stiles, "An Investigation of Children's Concept of Self-Responsibility for Their School Learning," American Educational Research Journal 13 (1976), 167. Quoted by Alfie Kohn, *Punished by Rewards* (New York, NY: Houghton Mifflin Company, 1993), 222.

4. Teresa M. Amabile and Judith Gitomer, "Children's Artistic Creativity: Effects of Choice in Task Materials," Personality and Social Psychology Bulletin 10 (1984). Quoted by Kohn, *Punished by Rewards,* 222.

5. Zuckerman, Miron et al., "On the Importance of Self-Determination for Intrinsically-Motivated Behavior," Personality and Social Psychology Bulletin 4 (1978). Quoted by Kohn, *Punished by Rewards,* 222.

6. Arthur K. Ellis and Jeffrey T. Fouts, *Research on Educational Innovations* (Larchmont, NY: Eye on Education, 1997), 64.

7. Barbara L. McCombs and Jo Sue Whisler, *The Learner-Centered Classroom and School* (San Francisco, CA: Jossey-Bass Inc., Publishers, 1997), 59-60.

CHAPTER NINE

FROM DRUDGERY TO DELIGHT

O ur son, Matt, hated math. He mightily resisted learning his multiplication facts. It was beginning to really affect his progress in fourth grade. We preached at him to study his multiplication tables. We bought flashcards for him. We installed a kids' math program on our family computer.

Nothing worked. Matt said, "I hate multiplication. It's boring."

He avoided studying and spent his time instead pursuing his latest craze—movie-making. He loved to make humorous videos with our camcorder. The star of the shows was usually Wild Thing, one of his old puppets. He drafted Thom to be the puppeteer and voice of Wild Thing. Matt created the sets, gathered the props, set up the lighting, roughed out the story lines, and ran the camera, while Dad became the rather obnoxious persona of this fuzzy creature.

During the taping sessions, Matt got so tickled that he couldn't contain himself, even though he was right next to the microphone as the cameraman. His laughter formed the audience laugh track on the tape. The recorded laughter only contributed to Matt's repeated laughter every time he watched his homespun comedies.

After starring in dozens and dozens of Wild Thing movies, Thom came upon an idea. He could see that Matt got such glee out of the Wild Thing comedies, spending hours and hours making them and watching them. On the other hand, Matt viewed his multiplication tables as drudgery, and therefore resisted spending any time on them. So finally Dad suggested that Wild Thing star in *The Merry Math Revue*. Matt loved the idea! He immediately went to work on the set and the props.

The *Revue* included plenty of fourth-grade humor centered around such things as toilet paper and belches. And, of course, it featured musical numbers with goofy lyrics that just happened to include all the multiplication facts. Matt howled in laughter. He watched that tape over and over and over, singing along with it every time.

Before he knew what had happened, he knew his multiplication tables. In math he went from a C student to an A student.

Let's analyze what happened here. Matt learned without use of a bribe. Thom never said, "Do this and you'll get that." He simply invited Matt to indulge in something Matt found delightful.

Matt became intrinsically motivated to make the video. Let's check out how the video experience fits the *REAL* learning formula for setting an intrinsically motivating environment.

Was it *relational?* Yes, it was a great father-and-son relational project. It was a fine time for sharing laughs and working toward a common goal.

Was it *experiential?* Yes, it was truly a hands-on, learn-by-doing active project. It involved multiple senses.

Was it *applicable?* Yes, in fact it provided two different life applications that Matt clearly understood. First, the work involved in making the project would result in a show he could watch over and over. And second, he knew his knowledge of the multiplication facts would help him in school and in everyday life.

Was it *learner-based?* Yes, the project began with what Matt liked. It matched his styles of learning. He made choices. He got to choose the character, the props, the story line. He was the director!

DELIGHT AND THE BRAIN

There's one more element that made this authentic learning project successful—*delight*. It tapped into what made Matt giggle. It made learning fun. Matt thoroughly enjoyed the process—and he learned what he needed to learn.

Matt is not unusual. His brain works like everybody's brain. What we see here is a common brain function. When an activity is enjoyable, fun, delightful, intriguing, and colorful, the brain says, "Wow! This is good stuff! We gotta save this!" And it does.

The authors of *The Learning Revolution* write: "Make [learning] outlandish, funny and preferably emotional—because the 'filter' in the brain that transfers information to your long-term memory is very closely linked with the brain's emotional center. And link your associations with as many senses as you can: sight, sound, smell, touch and taste."[1]

In Chapter 5 we explored the power of emotions in the learning process. We now know that delight is one of the most potent emotions for enhancing learning. People learn more and retain it longer when they enjoy the process. On the other hand, they learn less and forget it sooner when the learning environment seems boring or tedious.

> *"Emblazon these words on your mind:*
> *Learning is more effective when it's fun."*
>
> PETER KLINE, *THE EVERYDAY GENIUS*

Daniel Goleman, author of *Emotional Intelligence,* writes that good moods "enhance the ability to think flexibly and with more complexity, thus making it easier to find solutions to problems, whether intellectual or interpersonal." He cites a study which found that people who had just watched a video of television bloopers were more successful than those who hadn't seen the video at solving a typical puzzle used by psychologists to test creative thinking.[2]

Another study on delight is reported by Matt Weinstein in his book *Managing to Have Fun*. Researchers wanted to determine if any relationship existed between delight and the tendency to do good deeds. They had noticed that people generally sought and received delight when they found leftover coins in a pay telephone coin-return cup. Everybody gets a kick out of getting something for nothing! So the researchers began randomly planting coins in phone coin-return cups. Then they hired a young woman to walk by the phone at the exact moment the subjects checked the coin-return cup. Just as the woman walked by, she pretended to stumble and dropped her books on the ground.

Astonishingly, the researchers discovered that the people who found money in the coin return were *four times as likely* to stop and help the woman pick up her books than were the people who found no money.[3]

Delight is a powerful and positive emotion.

The Delight Bashers

Regardless of the scientific research and just plain common sense, delight still has a bad name among many educators and church leaders. "Learning is serious business" they say. "We're not here for a bunch of fun and games. We're here to learn."

Somehow enjoyment and learning have become mutually exclusive in many people's opinions. We've certainly heard those opinions since we created Hands-On Bible Curriculum, which comes packaged with colorful gizmos we use to engage children in learning activities. "That's not real curriculum," some traditionalist teachers sniff. "Where are the pupil worksheets? All I see is a bunch of toys!" If these teachers would hear laughter coming from a classroom, they'd likely assume no learning was occurring.

The gizmos are there because we've found they generate delight among young learners. Like Matt and Wild Thing, the delight-filled Hands-On activities encourage intrinsic motivation for children to learn important content. And laughter is encouraged as healthy evidence of delight.

Why have some people assumed learning and enjoyment don't mix? Part of the mind-set may be wrapped up in old work ethic notions. "Good workers work hard." The words *work* and *hard* connote a humorless sweat fest. And those words have been transferred over into educational settings—*work*sheet, home*work*, *work*shop, school*work*. Good students study *hard*, and they take *hard* classes. The work-related images of factories and production lines seem to have transferred as well. Just like an old factory, many schools and churches *work hard* to process students through like identical manufactured goods on a production line.

> *"In my 30 years of investigating people's association*
> *with the word 'study,'*
> *ten major words or concepts have emerged.*
> *They are: boring, exams, homework, waste of time,*
> *punishment, irrelevant, detention, 'yuck,' hate and fear."*
>
> TONY BUZAN, *MAKE THE MOST OF YOUR MIND*

Professor William Reinsmith of the Philadelphia College of Pharmacy and Science said, "Quite often—perhaps far more often than we can afford to admit—the classroom is an inappropriate context for genuine learning...The more learning is like play, the more absorbing it will be—unless the student has been so corrupted by institutional education that only dull, serious work is equated with learning. It is frightening how hard a teacher must work to convince today's college students that study and learning can be interesting—even joyful—activities."[4]

Many college faculty members themselves seem bent on maintaining the academic image as dull, humorless, stuffy, and oh-so-serious. Then, of course, their students absorb this image and carry away a bias that all learning is dull, humorless, stuffy, and oh-so-serious.

Somewhere along the line, the academic community (and much of the church) seems to have forgotten that one of the most important things to learn is a love for learning. Few people gain a love for anything that is marinated in drudgery.

People learn more—and learn to love learning—when they enjoy the process. But some "serious" church educators have told us, "Yes, but life isn't always fun. It isn't always interesting. And kids better learn to deal with that." The logic here seems to indicate that the basic goal of Christian education is not to get kids excited about the faith, but to acclimate them to doing dull busywork. Is that our goal?

We sometimes hear teachers and leaders say things such as, "OK, kids, fun time's over. It's time to study our Bibles." What message does that send about the Bible? How could a learner escape the implicit message that reading God's Word is a joyless chore, something to be avoided whenever the teacher isn't around?

JESUS AND DELIGHT

We have no indication that anyone ever characterized Jesus' teaching ministry as dull, boring, or stuffy. People found his message fascinating. And they needed no one forcing them to attend his sessions.

Jesus displayed a penchant to delight. Consider his first miracle—turning water into wine for the wedding at Cana. What a delightful feat! The master of the banquet was fascinated and delighted when he tasted Jesus' superb drink. "Everyone brings out the choice wine first and then the cheaper wine after the guests have had too much to drink; but you have saved the best till now" (John 2:10). What a fun way to top off a party.

Jesus definitely had a delightful flair for the sensational. Look how he told Peter to find some cash for the temple tax in Matthew 17:27. Jesus, the Son of God, could certainly have reached into his garment and produced a coin for Peter. But that would have generated little delight. Instead he told Peter to go to the lake and catch a fish. Inside the fish's mouth he would find a coin with which to pay the tax! How do you think Peter felt about that experience? Would he call that dry, colorless learning? Or do you suppose he experienced an unforgettable flash of delight?

> "A cheerful heart is good medicine,
> but a crushed spirit dries up the bones."
>
> PROVERBS 17:22

DEVELOPING DELIGHT

When it comes to learning about the greatest story ever told, fun is not to be feared. It's an asset! Delight will help your learners learn. It will make them eager to return for more. It will make them want to bring their friends.

We need to change the paradigm for learning in the church. The old paradigm would have us believe that a successful teacher or leader stands before a silent, motionless group of students. The new delight-oriented paradigm shows us a room full of engaged learners who are talking, smiling, and laughing while they discover God's truths.

The old paradigm evaluates Christian education by asking teachers, "Do you have your class under control?" The new paradigm asks learners, "Are you having fun? What did you enjoy most about today's lesson?" If learners are having fun while they're learning, their intrinsic motivation is engaged, creating an internal thirst to learn more and retain it longer.

How can we develop delight? We'll explore five ways: knowing your learners, leading by example, creating a sense of play, replacing bribes with surprises, and creating an environment of delight.

Know Your Learners

In order to develop delight, we must understand our learners and know what brings them delight. We must go out of our way to know their culture, know what makes them laugh, know what fascinates them.

In our research for vacation Bible school, we're always snooping around to discover the latest trends and developments that bring delight to children. One year it was little rockets that actually blasted off with the fizz power of Alka-Seltzer. For the Treasure Hunt Bible Adventure VBS we enabled kids to create Jungle Gel, a goo they made themselves. These were major delight producers that thematically tied into the biblical truths being explored by the kids.

Unfortunately, we sometimes hear from teachers and directors who see our field-tested ideas for such activities and refuse to use them. "Kids wouldn't like those things," they predict. But they haven't consulted the experts—the kids themselves. They don't know their learners. They can't bring delight if they cling to erroneous perceptions of what brings delight.

One of the more memorable examples of these erroneous perceptions came when we introduced the concept of allowing teams of kids at VBS to make the snacks for the entire group. "That'll never work," we were told by many teachers and directors. "Kids won't want to mess with that." Well, as usual, we weren't advocating a concept we hadn't tested with real kids in real churches. They love it! In fact many kids report their time in the kitchen is a highlight of the week for them. They get to put their faith into action serving others. Besides, the snacks are fun works of art. For example, to add thematic delight when they learned about Paul's voyages, kids made little boats from pita bread. Cheese triangles formed the sails. Paul himself was created from a pretzel with a grape head stuck on top. Delight-full!

Lead by Example

If we want to develop delight, we must be willing to model fun and delight to our learners. If an active-learning experience calls for everyone to take off their shoes and wiggle their toes, the teacher needs to lead the way. If a church needs to loosen up and become a happier place, the pastor needs to lead the way—perhaps by donning "Groucho" glasses during a sermon on the futility of worry.

Directors of Christian education can't simply ask their teachers to "lighten up" and begin injecting delight. Especially in an environment where delight has been missing, the leaders must personally take the initial steps to show the way. Once people see their leaders beginning to mix fun and learning, they'll give it a try.

Our friend Cindy Hansen knows how to lead the delight bandwagon. Whenever she delivers a note, book, memo, letter, or assignment to her associates, Cindy always attaches treats. And she writes handwritten notes that link her messages to the treats. She'll tape a stick of gum to a request for help, with a note saying, "Chew on this and let me know." When she asks a volunteer to read a thick book, she'll write, "I know this is a lot of bedtime reading, so here's a little bag of coffee beans to keep you going." Her recipients love getting assignments from Cindy! She models delight.

As the chief leaders around the Group Publishing offices, we try to model delight often. Thom, who loves shaking society's image of CEOs, records strange and quirky greetings on his voice mail—just for fun. Many people call his number just to hear his latest zany recording. Joani assumes the role of the Affirmation Empress. Whenever she spots someone doing something right, she delivers a fun little toy, or edible treat, or clever note. Displays of delight from leaders set the tone and free people to release their own delight.

CREATE A SENSE OF PLAY

Jesus devoted special attention to children during his ministry. But he did so at considerable risk. In Bible times, the adult society viewed children as bothersome distractions. When an important teacher such as Jesus spoke, the children were expected to stay out of the way. Look what happened in Matthew 19:13-14:

> "Then little children were brought to Jesus for him to place his hands on them and pray for them. But the disciples rebuked those who brought them. Jesus said, 'Let the little children come to me, and do not hinder them, for the kingdom of heaven belongs to such as these.'"

Earlier in Matthew we read, "I tell you the truth, unless you change and become like little children, you will never enter the kingdom of heaven" (Matthew 18:3). We gain a picture of a Lord who loves children and loves the nature of children. "Therefore, whoever humbles himself like this child is the greatest in the kingdom of heaven" (verse 4).

Part of that humble nature of children is their unabashed sense of play and their freeing ability to mix play and learning. That's how young children learn—through play. They're fearless explorers, poking their noses into everything around them, learning about their world. Every day is a new adventure. When they fall down, they get right back up and try again. Failure is a natural part of the playful process of learning. No big deal.

But gradually as they grow older, our society teaches them that learning is completely serious business. Failure is final. They're taught that learning is really the dry accumulation of facts parked in short-term memory to satisfy some teacher's test.

Colin Rose and Malcolm J. Nicholl write: "One reason children learn so well is that they haven't developed preconceptions of how they are supposed to learn. Also, they have not developed the notion that play and work are mutually exclusive activities. Play *is* an important part of the learning experience. When we enjoy learning, we learn better."[5]

Seminary dean Leonard Sweet preaches about the church's need to return to a sense of play. Constant references to the Christian life being *work* send the wrong message. He says he and his wife do not "work" at their marriage. They "play" at it! What a de-light-full perspective! He believes church leaders need to stop conducting so many *work*shops and begin offering *play*shops.

> *"The more I want to get something done,*
> *the less I call it work."*

RICHARD BACH

To create delight in your church, introduce a sense of play with learners of all ages. If you want your class to share their thoughts with the whole group, make a game of it. Toss out a ball or other soft object and ask whomever catches it to share. That person then tosses it to another, and so on. If you're studying the book of Job, use a bit of play to introduce the serious subject of suffering. Ask learners to "show and tell" about a scar somewhere on their bodies. (Obviously, you'll want to set a couple of game rules. Some scar locations are best left hidden.)

Play. Use games and other elements of delight to make learning playful.

REPLACE BRIBES WITH SURPRISES

Remember, we want to avoid the "do this and you'll get that" approach. We can encourage intrinsic motivation when we create an environment where unexpected surprises are welcome.

Our administrative assistant, Betty, helps us in so many ways. She's a true servant. And she could be a poster child for intrinsic motivation! We like to spread a little delight by surprising Betty now and then. One day we told her to grab her coat. "It's time for a little break," we said. We drove her to the mall, and once inside we handed her a crisp $100 bill. We told her, "You have thirty minutes to shop for whatever you want. Use this money to make your purchases. At the end of the thirty minutes you must be back here. Anything you buy is yours to keep. But any money you have leftover you have to return to us. So we suggest you get started!"

She dashed off like a crazed game-show contestant. She bolted into store after store, racing to any items that caught her eye. The store clerks were most bewildered by this shopper in a big hurry. With less than a minute to spare, she arrived back at our spot, carrying several sacks of goods. She managed to spend almost every dollar.

We laughed all the way back to the office. And Betty has never forgotten her delight-full surprise shopping spree.

Washington children's worker Sandi Wright was in the habit of rewarding her students with "Adventure Bucks" for reciting Scripture, bringing their Bibles, arriving on time, and so on. One time she offered a trip to McDonald's to the kids who had earned enough Adventure Bucks. As the children were boarding the bus, Sandi noticed one little boy standing back with a forlorn look on his face. "I can't go," he said. "This is my first time here. I don't have any of those bucks."

Sandi thought a moment, then said, "Get on board. You're a winner with us!" The little boy beamed.

"I've never won anything in my life," he chirped as stepped aboard the bus.

It was then Sandi realized her efforts at pitting kids against one another wasn't worth it. She changed her whole approach. She organized children into small groups to learn Scripture through songs, raps, and skits. At first some kids complained, "Where's my bucks?" But soon they began enjoying the learning activities for their own merit. And Sandi's occasional surprises added delight that helped keep intrinsic motivation high.

For many years Ohio youth worker Steve Huddleston dangled an annual "Youth Leadership Award" before his graduating teenagers. One student was singled out and recognized in front of the congregation. Recently Steve decided to change his approach. He surprised all the students and their parents by honoring *each* graduating senior in front of the congregation. Everyone was delighted!

CREATE AN ENVIRONMENT OF DELIGHT

Delight emerges more easily in places that look delight-full. How does your place look? Do you see signs of delight?

Our staff at Group Publishing manages to keep new signs of delight popping up all the time. One time several staffers came in after hours and assembled a complete eighteen-hole miniature golf course throughout the building. One of the holes required golfers to hit the ball into a cardboard cutout of Thom's gaping mouth. The staff loved it! Sure, everybody had to spend some time away from their work to try the course. But the delight factor helped them return to their jobs with renewed vigor and a sense of delight about their workplace.

At one point we acquired a new staff member, Dorothy. But she's a little cold. In fact, it's hard to find a pulse on Dorothy. That's because she's a mannequin. But Dorothy performs her job well. She spreads delight. When someone goes out on vacation, Dorothy sits at the person's desk. When meetings get a little long, somebody tosses in Dorothy to liven things up. When staffers want to give the night custodians a little surprise, they park her in a bathroom stall. Dorothy is now part of our delight environment.

Does your environment show evidence of delight? You can create a delight-full atmosphere in many ways. Decorate for delight. Bring in delight-full items such as a huge fishing net (it's biblical). Install a theater-style popcorn machine. Make big blowups of fun photographs from past church functions. Reserve a parking space with a sign reading, "Latecomers Only." Stock the church kitchen with big chef hats. Post baby pictures of church staff, and invite members to guess who's who.

Loosen up. Let your community know that your church values joy. Delight and joy are appropriate symbols of the church. People thirst for an environment of joy, of forgiveness, of grace, of delight. As Christians, if we don't "advertise" a modicum of joy, we shouldn't expect non-Christians to find us too attractive. "The peace that passes all understanding" ought to bring smiles to our faces.

When we advocate delight, we don't ask you to incorporate inappropriate stunts. You needn't be goofy or embarrassing. You choose the elements of delight that fit your particular church. Be delight-full in ways that fit you.

REFERENCES

1. Gordon Dryden and Jeannette Vos, *The Learning Revolution* (Rolling Hills Estates, CA: Jalmar Press, 1994), 169.

2. Daniel Goleman, *Emotional Intelligence* (New York, NY: Bantam Books, 1995), 85.

3. Matt Weinstein, *Managing to Have Fun* (New York, NY: Simon & Schuster, 1996), 49.

4. Colin Rose and Malcom J. Nicholl, *Accelerated Learning for the 21st Century* (New York, NY: Delacorte Press, 1997), 251-252.

5. Rose and Nicholl, *Accelerated Learning for the 21st Century,* 63.

Falling on Good Dirt

"Still other seed fell on good soil,
where it produced a crop—
a hundred, sixty or thirty times what was sown.

The one who received the seed
that fell on good soil
is the man who hears the word
and understands it.
He produces a crop, yielding a hundred,
sixty or thirty times what was sown."

MATTHEW 13:8, 23

Jesus brings us around to the real purpose of sowing. He's not interested in simply scattering seeds. He's not interested in simply pulling weeds. We see here Jesus' singularity of purpose. It's the crop.

After four different tries, the crop now succeeds. Throughout the different scenarios, good seed was sown. The same seed was sown. And throughout the four scenarios, we see a good sower—the same sower. But this sower witnessed four very different results. Only the final attempt resulted in a crop.

Our story concludes on a farm with good soil that produces a successful crop. For every seed sown, we see a yield of thirty, sixty, or one hundred times what was sown. Some Bible scholars say a yield of ten to one was considered a fine crop in Jesus' day. This yield of thirty, sixty, or one hundred times was spectacular! Why did this planting work so well?

Jesus tells us that the fourth field consisted of good soil. Its consistency, condition, preparation, and maintenance were such that the tender seed flourished. He tells us the receiver of this seed did more than hear the Word. He *understood* it. He didn't simply go through the motions. The conditions were such that the Word made sense to him personally.

Once the Word was truly understood by the hearer, look what happened. It was multiplied by thirty, sixty, or one hundred times. Talk about growth! What would happen in your church if you saw a yield like that? Can you imagine the impact of growing by a factor of thirty, sixty, or one hundred?

PREPARING THE FIELDS

Bud knows about good dirt. He's been farming so long that he can just eyeball a field and tell if it will produce a good crop.

Good, highly productive fields are not accidents. In order to produce good yields, a field requires work. It requires preparation before the planting ever begins. Bud makes the extra effort to work the ground in the fall. "It makes it easier for the little seeds to grow in the spring," he says.

There's a lesson here for us. If we care about a good yield, we need to prepare the ground ahead of time. It's worth the effort. It affects the crop.

Bud knows how to get the most out of his fields. His yields often surpass those of the fields right across the road. How does he do that year after year? We were able to squeeze one more secret out of him. This secret also holds great promise for the church. He describes it this way:

"We're willing to try new ideas.
Last year we worked twenty-four different test plots.
If one beats what we did last year, we'll switch."

Here's a man who's been farming for fifty years. You'd think that someone who's had the same task for a half century might easily get set in his ways. But not Bud. He's always looking for a better way. He's open to change. He knows that fresh ideas can make a substantial impact on his yield. So he doesn't cling to the old ways. He doesn't pine for "the good old days." He knows a great farmer plows his field by looking forward.

Are you stuck in your ways? Or are you ready to try some new things that could substantially increase your yield?

CHAPTER TEN

SIGNS OF A SUCCESSFUL CROP

T he "good dirt" person hears the Word, understands it, and produces a big crop. People can hear this parable a hundred times—and miss the point. The point here is the crop—the results!

Jesus is results-oriented. When thinking about this parable, or about ministry, if we focus on the seed, we miss the point. The purpose of God's Word isn't merely to exist, or to be heard, or even to sprout. It's the crop! The purpose of a sower isn't merely to sow, or to sow with precision. It's the crop!

This is the parable's message for the church. We can preach with fervor; we can teach with eloquence; we can witness with passion. But if we evaluate our effort on any of those criteria, we miss the point. That's not it. What matters are the *results* of our effort.

We often begin our workshops by asking participants to think about the desired long-term results of learning in the church. We ask, "What's the goal of Christian education? What do you wish to instill in your learners that will affect their lives long after they leave you?" Our audiences of educators, youth workers, children's directors, pastors, and Christian education directors usually come up with a fine list of objectives. They mention things such as

- a close relationship with Jesus Christ,
- a commitment to serving others,
- living a Christian lifestyle, and
- being "salt and light" to the world.

Here's what's interesting. In all the times we've done this exercise with church leaders, no one has ever said his or her long-term goal for learners was for them to remember the ten plagues of Egypt, or to recite 1 Corinthians 13, or to know the name of the king at the time the Magi visited the Christ child.

We find this unsettling, because there seems to be a gaping chasm between what we want and what we are doing. We say we want our learners to bear real fruit, but we spend so much of our time in activity that seems to bear little resemblance to the process of bearing that kind of fruit.

To get a different perspective, one could ask a similar question of parents. "What kind of person do you want your child to become?" Parents often say things such as "happy," "caring," "giving," "a contributing member of society." How do most good parents go about instilling those values? Do they ask their children to find the word "caring" in a word-search puzzle? Do they hand their teenagers a worksheet with a fill-in-the-blank sentence such as, "I will become a contributing _____ of society"?

No. We believe effective parents are more results-oriented. They spend their time in ways that lead directly to the qualities they desire for their children. If they want little Susie to share with her brother, they don't stick a worksheet in front of her or require her to memorize an essay on sharing. They help her understand the concept of sharing, the need for it, and the benefits of it. And they help her experience the concept with her brother, right on the spot. Those actions help lead to a sharing person. That's the goal, the desired result.

It seems so obvious. But for centuries we've missed the point. That's probably why Jesus saw the need to share the Parable of the Sower with us. He wants to focus our attention on the results, the fruit. That's what matters.

Understanding First

"The one who received the seed that fell on good soil is the man who hears the word and understands it" (Matthew 13:23a). Hearing the Word is not good enough. Our people must *understand* it. The parable indicates that understanding is a prerequisite to bearing fruit.

First we must make sure our learners understand the Word. Hearing is not enough. Reading is not enough. Memorizing is not enough. Jesus shows us through this parable that we can easily get derailed if we don't understand the importance of understanding.

Other examples also illustrate how Jesus places understanding as a prerequisite for bearing fruit. Look at the colorful story of Jesus' healing of the demon-possessed man in Mark 5:1-20. Here Jesus encounters a frightening man who stumbles out of the tombs. Jesus commands the demons to leave the man. They promptly dash into two thousand pigs that then commit suicide in the lake. Wow! Spectacular! But what was the fruit? What was the desired result? We see the result in verses 18-20:

> "As Jesus was getting into the boat, the man who had been demon-possessed begged to go with him. Jesus did not let him, but said, 'Go home to your family and tell them how much the Lord has done for you.' So the man went away and began to tell in the Decapolis how much Jesus had done for him. And all the people were amazed."

Jesus wanted this man to understand. And he wanted the man's family to understand. The seeds sown this day no doubt yielded a crop thirty, sixty, or one hundred times what was sown. Because the man understood who Jesus was and what he had done for him, he spread the word to the ten Gentile cities of the

Decapolis—so that they too would understand.

Look also at Jesus' lesson in the washing of the disciples' feet. What does he say when Peter resists the foot bath? "You do not realize now what I am doing, but later you will understand" (John 13:7). Even though Peter started out a little confused, Jesus used this memorable learning experience to help his followers understand his message. Understanding the message of humble servanthood was a prerequisite of these men producing a high-yield crop.

Understanding the message leads to acting on the message, which leads to results. Jesus mentioned understanding quite often. Here are some other examples:

- "Have you understood all these things?" (Matthew 13:51).
- "Listen and understand" (Matthew 15:10b).
- "Do you still not understand?" (Matthew 16:9a).
- "Let the reader understand" (Matthew 24:15b).
- "Then he opened their minds so they could understand the Scriptures" (Luke 24:45).

As we see in the ministry of Jesus, understanding leads to faith and action. Faith in Jesus Christ is not borne of mindless ritual or of mesmerizing mantra. Faith in Christ is a thinking thing. It comes from understanding. But this understanding is within everyone's grasp. Jesus said, "I tell you the truth, anyone who will not receive the kingdom of God like a little child will never enter it" (Mark 10:15). The understanding of a child can lead to faith and fruit.

Understanding comes first. Without it we're fruitlessly casting seeds on the hard-packed path, on rocky ground, and among the thorns.

WHAT IS THE CROP?

The parable tells of a great yield of one hundred, sixty, or thirty times what was sown. What is this yield? What is the crop for those who teach? Is it a chart full of students' gold stars? Is it a recited verse? Is it a completed worksheet?

Farmer Bud knows why he plants, why he cultivates, why he weeds. His time is focused on the harvest, the crop. He invests so much time and care all for the end result. And that result can be measured two ways—quantitatively and qualitatively. He cares about his bushels per acre and about the quality of the harvested grain.

We can look at our task in a similar way. Our yield in the church can be measured both quantitatively and qualitatively. We should care about the number of souls who share a relationship with the Lord. And we should care about the quality, depth and expression of those individuals' faith.

We see an example of fruit quality in Galatians 5:22-23a:

> "But the fruit of the Spirit is love, joy, peace, patience, kindness, goodness, faithfulness, gentleness and self-control."

Examine these crops of the Spirit. Is it enough to simply preach them? Are we effective teachers if learners can recite the fruit of the Spirit? How does one know these qualities exist in a person? Do they not need to be put into practice to verify their existence, to be of value?

> *"It is not enough*
> *to lecture children about values:*
> *they need to practice them."*
>
> DANIEL GOLEMAN, *EMOTIONAL INTELLIGENCE*

Again, it seems so obvious. But in the church we manage to look past the obvious with unsettling frequency. We spend a lot of time preaching. But how much time do we devote for learners to practice what we preach?

Giving learners opportunities to practice God's Word develops understanding of the Word, and it shows evidence of the yield. But it seems we become all too tempted to sow, sow, sow, while disregarding the action the seed requires to grow into a mature plant that will produce fruit.

A few years ago we attended an adult Bible study class that was led by the church's pastor. The theme for the day was prayer. The pastor provided a fine, detailed exegesis of the appropriate Bible passages. Toward the end of the session, a woman in the class shared that she had been served with lawsuit papers earlier that morning. The trembling in her voice telegraphed her fear and uncertainty over the situation. She was very vulnerable in front of this class of twenty people. The pastor, perhaps with an intent to lighten up a tense moment, chuckled and said, "Those deputies—delivering a summons on a Sunday morning! They should be in church." He then went back to his teaching: "We read in James 5:16 that we should 'pray for each other so that you may be healed.' Now this was near the end of James' letter. . ." He charged right ahead, casting seeds.

The pastor missed the point. He didn't get it. Here, into his lap, plopped a most appropriate learning and ministry opportunity. But he was preoccupied with teaching. Here was a woman who needed the kind of prayer that James wrote about. And here was a class that could have practiced the power of prayer right then and there. But the pastor wanted to sow.

You see, because the church has focused almost entirely on *teaching*, we miss the obvious. We don't think about *learning*. We don't think about giving learners the opportunity to *practice* what they're learning—right then and there. Practice helps learners *understand* the message. And understanding leads to *results*.

Results require understanding. Understanding requires results. Results are the crop.

In our book *Why Nobody Learns Much of Anything at Church: And How to Fix It,* we posed a crop question:

> Which of the following would best indicate to you that a student has learned the parable of the Good Samaritan?
> A. The student memorizes and recites the entire parable word for word from your preferred translation.
> B. The student tells the parable in his or her own words.
> C. The student explains an example of someone being a "good Samaritan."
> D. The student decides to sit and have lunch with an outcast kid who's rumored to have AIDS.[1]

When we focus on results, it changes our entire approach to education. The educator's success depends on the crop.

Assessing the Yield

When it comes to educational results, the crop yield, the church seems to have two problems. The first is remembering that the harvest is indeed the goal. The second is building mechanisms to measure the harvest, to make sure the yield is indeed satisfactory.

For Bud, focusing on the harvest and measuring the harvest seem to come naturally. He wouldn't operate any other way. But the church often seems preoccupied with other things. Perceived effectiveness in the church is based on other things, such as coverage of material, completion of student worksheets, number of verses memorized, orderliness of the students, and contentment of the teachers. If that's what we're using to determine educational effectiveness, the lessons in the Parable of the Sower tell us we'll never harvest a crop.

Rather than quantifying the seeds and the sowing, why shouldn't the church measure the real crop—how much learners learn, how much they retain, how they apply their learning to their everyday lives, and how many new learners come on board?

The public education establishment uses the word *assessment* to describe academic measurement. Let's analyze assessment. What's the purpose of assessment? Many people believe assessment evaluates students' performance. They believe assessment's primary value is to judge and compare the students' efforts. We take a different view. We contend that assessment's main purpose and value in the church is to evaluate the teacher's and the curriculum's performance. If the crop yield is high, we want to encourage more of the same from the teachers and the curriculum. If the yield is low, it's time to make some changes with the teachers and the curriculum.

Mary Jane Drummond, in her book *Learning to See,* writes, "Effective assessment is a process in which our understanding of [students'] learning, acquired through observation and reflection, can be used to evaluate and enrich the curriculum we offer."[2]

Assessment is crucial to increasing our yield. The operating discipline of the Parable of the Sower is assessment. Jesus makes his big point by revealing the yield—thirty, sixty, one hundred times what was sown. The successful strategy of planting seeds in good soil is verified by the assessment of the yield. That assessment encourages us to do more planting in good soil.

What to Assess

We addressed earlier the problems of teaching facts in the absence of understanding the meaning. The problem of teaching mere facts is compounded when we focus assessment on short-term memory of mere facts. That assessment sends the message to learners and teachers that fact-collecting is the real goal. It must be, because that's what's measured! But Jesus makes clear in the Parable of the Sower that understanding, not mere fact-collecting, leads to real results.

Our schools struggle with similar issues concerning what to assess. Lorna M. Earl and Paul G. LeMahieu wrote a piece called "Rethinking Assessment and Accountability" for public school teachers and administrators. Here's an excerpt:

> The prevailing beliefs about knowledge and learning were consistent with a manufacturing approach. Knowledge was considered to be . . . *stuff* that had to be shifted from one location (e.g., teachers' minds, textbooks, chalkboards) to where it was supposed to go (i.e., students' heads). The obvious instructional approaches were things like drill and practice, recitation, and worksheets. Assessment focused on recall, reconstruction, and repetition of learned material. Standards for judgment amounted to identical correspondence between the taught material and its reproduction in the testing situation. As the world has changed, the factory model is proving to be inadequate.[3]

Asking fact-based questions does not give us helpful assessment information about a learner's ability to bear fruit. And asking a student to merely parrot a Scripture passage does not tell us about his or her depth of understanding nor application of the Word. We need to assess for understanding and application.

Mary Drummond reveals another interesting problem with quizzing children about mere facts. She writes:

> They [students] are skilled at using all the clues available from the teacher's face, body and tone of voice, and they are amazingly quick to change their minds if the teacher indicates, however unwittingly, that their first response was incorrect. We have no chance of learning about children's learning if our questions focus on their performance in a highly predictable question and answer routine. We must not underestimate children's ability to divine the required answer without any mental activity corresponding to the learning we believe we are assessing."[4]

How to Assess

To determine the yield of our crop, we need to find ways to assess what's really important. We need to assess understanding of God's Word, retention of the learning, and life application.

One of our best methods of assessment is observation of learner behavior. After a lesson on compassion, do we see evidence of compassionate acts by our learners? After a lesson on forgiveness, do we hear about students forgiving one another, or their friends, or family members?

Do we hear evidence of understanding and retention of previous lessons? Michigan teacher Lynda Freeman taught a Hands-On Bible Curriculum lesson to fifth-graders on the theme of "fads come and go, but Jesus Christ lasts forever." One of the girls in the class had been saving her money to buy a Beanie Baby doll. Weeks after the Bible lesson, the girl told Lynda, "You know, I spent a bunch of money on a Beanie Baby. But that's just a fad. What really matters is my relationship with Jesus." That's a quality assessment of understanding, retention, and application.

Let's look at a number of ways you can assess for understanding, retention, and application.

1. **OBSERVATION.** Watch learners' behavior for examples of learned lessons.

2. **VERBAL RESPONSES.** Ask learners what they've learned. Do it right after a lesson and do it several weeks later.

3. **WRITTEN RECORDS.** Have learners write prayer journals, letters, or class newsletters. Check their learning from their work.

4. **DRAWING.** Have learners sketch Bible stories, murals, or cartoon strips.

5. **PRODUCTS.** Make a real-life extension of the learning. Doing a lesson on giving? Have learners work together to create a project where they actually give to needy people.

6. **SELF-EVALUATION TOOLS.** Give learners the same rating scale at the beginning and end of the year. Have them evaluate how they've grown spiritually, what contributed to their growth, and areas where they can continue to grow.

7. **PORTFOLIOS.** Keep files of learners' work that display their learnings. Send the files home quarterly to have parents review with the student his or her progress, sign a form, and return the portfolio to the church.

8. **TEACHER-STUDENT CONFERENCES.** This can be as simple as

taking a student out for ice cream and asking basic questions, such as "What have you learned this quarter that made a difference in your life?"

9. **PARENT-TEACHER-STUDENT CONFERENCES.** At the beginning of the year, meet, discuss, and note mutual expectations of the class. At the end of the year, review these notes to affirm and celebrate the growth that's occurred.

10. **SMALL-GROUP CONFERENCES.** Have groups of no more than four learners assess their growth together. Give them three or four guiding questions for evaluation, such as "How well did we accomplish the objective?"

11. **JOURNALS.** Have learners each keep a journal. Divide the pages into two sections— "What I Have Learned" and "Future Goals."

12. **CLASS SCRAPBOOK.** Take action photos of learners. Have learners tape the pictures in the scrapbook along with comments about how they've applied God's Word to their lives.

13. **FAITH HISTORY PROJECT.** Have learners chronicle their faith histories through photos, dates of important events, letters from people who've watched them grow spiritually, and written observations.

14. **VIDEO PROJECTS.** Have learners create videos that integrate lesson objectives, such as acting out modern-day parables.

15. **AUDIO PROJECTS.** At the beginning of the year, interview and record each learner with ten questions that reflect things he or she

should learn, such as "Who is God?" At the end of the year, use the same questions and tape. Have learners listen to and comment on the differences.

16. **LIVING BIBLE MUSEUM.** Have learners dress as Bible characters they've studied, create environments for Bible stories, and design interactive exhibits (what a plague of frogs would've felt like). Have learners be Bible character tour guides and lead other classes through the museum.

17. **STORY BOX.** Have each learner fill a box with items that a Bible character may have owned or used. Then have students take turns showing their boxes and guessing their Bible character.

18. **DRAMATIC PRESENTATION.** Let learners incorporate things they've learned by preparing and presenting any kind of drama, such as a pantomime, musical, or one-act play.

19. **LIVING BIBLE VERSES.** At the beginning of a unit, give learners a list of Bible verses that they need to "live out" outside of class. Have each learner and his or her parent sign a form confirming when each verse has been applied and how.

20. **INDIVIDUALIZED EDUCATIONAL PROGRAMS.** On a sheet of paper, list a learner's needs, your plans to help that child grow in those areas, and how you'll know if you've accomplished your objective. Regularly pray over each learner's program, and evaluate your progress toward accomplishing the goals.

21. **TEACHER FOR A DAY.** After a unit, have learners work in teams to develop a lesson on the topic for younger learners. Then

have them present their lesson to you and ultimately teach it to a younger class.

22. **MUSIC.** Have learners create a song that represents things they've learned. Have learners teach their song to the congregation.

23. **SHOW AND TELL.** Have learners each bring an object from home that illustrates the lesson's objective. For example, if students have learned about their importance in the body of Christ, a learner may bring an instrument to illustrate she can offer her musical gifts.

24. **ROLE PLAY.** After a unit, present scenarios that require application of the lesson's content. Then have learners work together to role play solutions to the problem.

25. **"WHY?" CIRCLE.** Have no more than four students sit in a circle. Have one learner make a comment about something he or she believes about God. Have other group members ask "Why?" until the learner has nothing more to say. Continue around the circle with each student stating a belief.

There are many methods to authentically assess your people's learning. Select the ways that work for you and your people. The important thing is to get started. Assess for understanding, retention, and application. Your purpose is not to determine which students are bright and dull. Your purpose, as in the parable, is to determine how your sowing might change to avoid hard-packed paths, rocky soil, and thorny weeds.

If your pastor would simply ask congregation members, "What do you remember from last week's sermon?" and "How did that message affect your life this past week?" we assure you the preaching in your church would take on a new face.

If your teachers would simply ask their learners, "What do you remember from last week's lesson?" and "How have you put that learning into practice this past week?" we assure you their teaching would quickly become more effective. They'd more likely support selecting a curriculum that exemplifies authentic learning. And your church will begin to see yields of thirty, sixty, one hundred times what was sown.

Preparing for a Bountiful Harvest

Bud's yields are greater today than they were in years past. In fact, today when he plants corn, he see yields of five hundred to one! That's not because he's working harder, longer hours. He'll tell you the reason is change and his own willingness to embrace change.

Some people view farmers as old-fashioned simpletons who work in the dirt. Farming may be the oldest profession in the world, but today's high-yield farmers are not old-fashioned. They operate efficient high-tech operations. Their equipment and agricultural techniques are completely up to date. Earth-orbiting satellites guide their tractors to maximize their time and utilization of the land.

Bud scours the technology-laden agricultural magazines for the latest tips on equipment and practices that will make his operation more productive. Every time we visit him, he shows us some new device, implement, tractor, or technique that enables him to increase his yield. He welcomes the changes in his life's calling.

Are you open to change? Is your church ready to embrace the changes necessary to increase your yield? We sometimes get discouraged when we ask those questions. In fact, a few years ago we surveyed Christian education directors. We asked, "If you found a new curriculum that you determined was more effective than what you're using now, would you switch?" This is a simple question about yield. Only 29 percent of the respondents said they would change.

For years we've been working to create tools to help churches increase their yield. These curricula and learning resources, distributed through Group Publishing, incorporate the elements that make up authentic learning. They emphasize these qualities:

- learner-based philosophy
- focus on understanding
- a thinking approach
- long-term retention
- genuine active learning
- learner-to-learner talk and discovery
- interval reinforcement
- equipping families for authentic learning
- bribe-free teaching
- intrinsic motivation
- delight
- learner-to-learner relationship-building
- absence of word puzzles, scrambles and fill-in-the-blanks
- emphasis on life application
- tools for assessment

These attributes combine to make what we call authentic learning materials. This innovative combination of qualities is revolutionary—and unique. We believe authentic learning is to the church what the computer is to the workplace. Can you remember the days of the typewriter? Different manufacturers jockeyed for the favor of customers. Manufacturers such as IBM, Royal, and

Remington boasted they offered the best typewriters. Some were incrementally superior to others. But then the personal computer came onto the scene. For work productivity and effectiveness, the computer offered a quantum leap above any typewriter. The desktop computer was a true breakthrough.

Likewise, authentic learning materials represent a true breakthrough. Sure, some claim to offer one or more of the authentic learning qualities. But until suppliers and users understand and embrace the total change needed to make the leap to authentic learning, partial attempts are akin to attaching a computer mouse to a typewriter. A casual observer may mistake a mousy typewriter for a powerful computer. But the performance, the yield, will tell the story.

The new learning technology is here today. God is counting on each of us to use what we've been given to prepare for a bountiful harvest. We disappoint God when we fail to take advantage of opportunities to increase our yield. Look at Jesus' Parable of the Talents (Matthew 25:14-30). Here a man entrusted varying amounts of money to three servants before he left on a journey. When he returned, he discovered that two of the servants doubled the investment entrusted to them. But one servant simply stashed the master's money in the ground.

Some would say the third servant performed satisfactorily. He didn't lose the money, waste it, or risk it. He kept it safe and guarded. But the master was unimpressed. He said, "Throw that worthless servant outside, into the darkness, where there will be weeping and gnashing of teeth" (Matthew 25:30). That servant did not appreciate that the master was interested in results, in yield, in growth. He thought simply maintaining the status quo would get him by. But that "safe" strategy evoked the raging ire of the master.

What about you? Are you comfortable with the safe, old strategies of yesteryear? Or are you ready to embrace the change necessary to produce a yield of thirty, sixty, one hundred or even five hundred times what you sow?

REFERENCES

1. Thom and Joani Schultz, *Why Nobody Learns Much of Anything at Church: And How to Fix It* (Loveland, CO: Group Publishing, 1993), 21.

2. Mary Jane Drummond, *Learning to See* (York, ME: Stenhouse Publishers, 1994), 13.

3. Lorna M. Earl and Paul G. LeMahieu, "Rethinking Assessment and Accountability," *1997 ASCD Yearbook* (Alexandria, VA: Association for Supervision and Curriculum Development, 1997), 161.

4. Drummond, *Learning to See,* 94-95.

WHERE DO WE GROW FROM HERE?

Y ou've just finished this book.

Hopefully you're challenged to plant seeds of change in your own church now. But how? You can't do it alone. Follow these steps toward change and see the incredible things God will do through you!

STEP 1: BECOME THE CHAMPION

That's *you!* If God has spoken to you through the words on these pages, you are the champion of the cause to transform learning in your church. Realize champions don't just make it on their own. They have supporters. And God is your greatest and most ardent fan! Go to God in prayer and find strength in the same power that rose Jesus Christ from the grave. That same mighty power is and will be working in you! (Check out Ephesians 1:15-20 for reassurance.)

Also know that we will be praying for you. We pray that God will give you the courage, patience, and vision it takes to bring about much-needed change. We believe God will do great things through people like you who trust in God and want his Word to come alive in people's lives.

Pray that God helps you see the people in your life who can come alongside you as you spread the vision. That's next!

STEP 2: ENLIST THE CORE

Find two to six other people who you believe share your passion for learning in the church. This small group will become the next step in facilitating change. Prayerfully consider people who have a desire to see God's Word take root in others' lives in fresh and exciting ways.

Maybe they'll be other Christian educators, pastors, teachers, or concerned parents. Review a list of church members, Bible study leaders, Sunday school teachers, church leadership, people of any age (for example, teenagers, senior citizens, young adults). Select open-minded people committed to revolutionizing the church, people who understand change.

Who might those people be? Jot down your ideas here:

_____

_____

_____

_____

_____

_____

_____

_____

Once you've compiled a list of core people, contact them and share your vision and the potential you see for your church. Ask your "core" to make these commitments:

a. **READ THIS BOOK.**

(Get more copies through your local Christian bookstore or from Group Publishing, 1515 Cascade Ave., Loveland, CO 80538.)

b. **JOIN YOU IN A BREAKFAST DISCUSSION GROUP FOR FOUR WEEKS** to discuss the concepts in this book. (There's nothing magical about breakfast—it's just a suggestion!)

c. **HELP FORMULATE A FOLLOW-UP PLAN.** Once you've talked about how the principles in this book could apply to your church, discuss questions such as these:

- What is our church's vision and mission for education?
- How could our church benefit from implementing the concepts in this book?
- What would have to change for things to be different in our church?
- What challenges would we face? (people, space, time, money?)
- Who are the key people we would need to train and "bring on board"?
- What other issues need to be addressed?
- When can we bring people together for the next step?

Once you've answered those questions, you're ready to meet the challenge!

STEP 3: ACCEPT THE CHALLENGE

You're now ready to bring more people into your plan for change. You and your core are ready to train others.

Make sure you have key church leadership on board. For example, if you're not the pastor, contact the pastor and share what you hope to accomplish through your vision of Christian education. If your core group wasn't made up of educational leadership from the church, communicate to the existing educational leadership what you'd like to do.

We don't call this "The Challenge" for nothing! Be prepared for people feeling uncomfortable with rattling the status quo. Continue to pray for God's guidance throughout the process. (We've heard countless stories of churches that were hesitant, even hostile to the idea of change. But once people understood the rationale and motive for changing unfruitful habits, God blessed their efforts beyond their wildest dreams! Many churches willing to change have reported unprecedented growth in their educational programs—plus families are joining their churches because of the exciting things happening!)

To make your training job easier, we've put together *The Dirt on Learning* Training Kit. This kit contains four ninety-minute training sessions complete with lesson plans, video clips of actual classroom footage and interviews, overhead transparencies, and a few surprises. In addition, you can purchase multiple copies of this book at a special rate.

Publicize the training sessions. We believe people will be delighted with the fast-paced and engaging sessions. They'll also enjoy the time for reflection and personal discovery.

Teach the sessions yourself, or assign someone to help you. Just follow the step-by-step guide for a no-fail learning adventure!

Remember, you're not alone. We want to be there for you. If you have any questions or concerns, please e-mail us. Addresses:

tschultz@grouppublishing.com
jschultz@grouppublishing.com

Check out our Web site just for this book:

(http://www.grouppublishing.com/dirt).

STEP 4: IMPLEMENT THE CHANGE

With other people trained in understanding how learning in the church can transform people's lives, you and your church may be faced with many changes.

It's possible that you'll have changes in teaching personnel. It's possible you'll have changes in curriculum resources. It's possible you may have changes in space needs (even how you arrange classroom furniture!).

Keep communication lines open and watch for growth—not only in spiritual depth, understanding, and life application, but in numbers too! Remember, as Paul says, "I can do all things through Christ who strengthens me" (Philippians 4:13, New King James Version)!

Group Publishing, Inc.
Attention: Product Development
P.O. Box 481 ● Loveland, CO 80539
Fax: (970) 679-4370

Evaluation for *THE DIRT ON LEARNING*

Please help Group Publishing, Inc., continue to provide innovative and useful resources for ministry. Please take a moment to fill out this evaluation and mail or fax it to us. Thanks!

● ● ●

1. As a whole, this book has been (circle one)

not very helpful   very helpful

1   2   3   4   5   6   7   8   9   10

2. The best things about this book:

3. Ways this book could be improved:

4. Things I will change because of this book:

5. Other books I'd like to see Group publish in the future:

6. Would you be interested in field-testing future Group products and giving us your feedback? If so, please fill in the information below:

Name _____

Street Address _____

City _____ State _____ ZIP _____

Phone Number _____ Date _____

GROW FAITH IN YOUR CHURCH — IN EVERY CLASSROOM!

The Dirt on Learning Video Training Kit

This thought-provoking video training kit from veteran educators Thom & Joani Schultz explores what Jesus' Parable of the Sower says about effective teaching and learning. The kit will enable you to take the truths learned in the book and turn them into a dynamic presentation for your entire church staff. You will be able to challenge and inspire your ministry team and set a practical course of action for positive change. Your teachers will re-think the Christian education methods currently in use, and consider what really works!

The kit includes the book, training video, 7 overhead transparencies, a leader's guide with reproducible handouts, seed packets, and magazine subscription discounts.

ISBN 0-7644-2152-2 $149.99

Why Nobody Learns Much of Anything at Church: And How to Fix It

Thom & Joani Schultz

Research shows there's no shortage of teaching in the church, but there is an alarming shortage of learning. In this book, you'll explore 10 keys to help unlock learning in your church. You won't find any easy fixes—just tested, solid, and creative approaches that focus on learning, not teaching. Plus, you get step-by-step ideas and plans for making real changes. Get the book to do an in-depth study of the Christian education programs at your church!

Softcover book	ISBN 1-55945-907-7	$12.99
Paperback book	ISBN 1-55945-902-6	$5.99
Spanish version book	ISBN 1-55945-663-9	$10.99

Extraordinary Results From Ordinary Teachers

Michael D. Warden

Perfect for teachers of every age level! Now both professional and volunteer Christian educators can teach as Jesus taught! You'll explore the teaching style and methods of Jesus and get clear and informed ways to deepen your teaching and increase your impact! Essential for every pastor and teacher of children through adults.

3 4711 00149 3875   0-7644-2013-5 $16.99

Order today from your local Christian bookstore, or write:
Group Publishing, P.O. Box 485, Loveland, CO 80539.